C000259982

SOFT SKILLS FOR LAWYERS

Giuseppe Giusti

Chelsea Publishing
—— London ——

First Edition published 2008 by Chelsea Publishing.

ISBN 978-0-9558926-0-8

Chelsea Publishing Limited
12 Olive Court
Liverpool Road
London N1 0RQ
United Kingdom
www.chelseapublishing.com

Cover by John Waller (www.johnwaller.co.uk)

Printed in Great Britain by the MPG Books Group, Bodmin and King's Lynn

TABLE OF CONTENTS

FORWARD AND ACKNOWLEDGEMENTS

Writing and publishing this book was a team effort. I would like to thank the many people who helped me to make it possible. Among these, Paul Buchan, who contributed to the editing and formatting of the book; Lauren Ellison, who wrote certain sections on dressing finesse; and John Waller, who kindly provided the picture that appears on the front cover.

I would also like to thank the many authors who have researched and written on the topics covered by this book before me and on whose books, articles and publications this book is based. A list of these authors, books and publications is provided in the bibliography and further reading section at the end of this book, to which readers are encouraged to refer for all purposes.

Finally, I would like to thank the readers themselves for their interest in this publication and praise them for their willingness to invest their time and energy to further improve themselves, both from a personal and a professional perspective. I hope that this book will contribute to your professional and personal growth.

If you like this book, or if you learn something new by reading it, I would be grateful if you could recommend it to your colleagues and friends and let me have any comments you might have by e-mailing team@chelseapublishing.com. Your support and comments will be an encouragement for all of us to keep working on similar projects in future.

Giuseppe Giusti
17 March 2008

CHAPTER 1 – INTRODUCTION TO SOFT SKILLS

1. Definition of Soft Skills

There has been a lot of talking recently in the legal profession about soft skills. A number of articles emphasising the importance of soft skills for lawyers have appeared in the legal press; a number of large City firms have introduced courses and programmes to offer their lawyers and partners basic training in soft skills; and a number of consulting and coaching organisations have started to market their services in this area to individual lawyers and law firms.

But what are soft skills and why are they important to the legal profession?

Soft skills are generally defined as those skills that influence how we interact with people. They include, at the most basic level, such abilities as effective communication, leadership, team building and listening skills and, at a more sophisticated level, such abilities as career planning, marketing and sales pitches, project management and delegation, public speaking and time management.

Soft skills are generally contrasted to technical skills or "hard skills", a category that includes, so far as lawyers are concerned, skills such as knowledge of the law and legal practice, legal analysis, legal research, legal drafting, business knowledge and so on.

The corporate world, particularly in the United States, has been reaping the benefits of training in soft skills for some time now. CEOs and senior managers in large corporations have long recognised that the higher a person rises in an organisation, the more they are required to effectively employ in their job skills such as communication, leadership and team building and take full responsibility for the development of their firm's business. That is why business leaders are taking advantage of soft skills training and enjoying significant returns.

1

The legal profession, by contrast, has only recently become aware of the importance of soft skills and the need to employ soft skills effectively, in a legal environment, when dealing with existing or potential clients and, within a firm, when dealing with superiors, colleagues, more junior lawyers, paralegals and other staff.

The high-end section of the legal world appears to have now recognised that in order for a lawyer to be successful in their career (and profitable for their firm) they need to master and employ effectively both soft skills and technical skills. As a consequence, a number of the largest City firms now offer their lawyers and partners the opportunity to attend courses and programmes that provide basic training in soft skills.

The breadth of these courses and programmes, however, still varies from firm to firm and only a few firms offer broad and all encompassing programs.

2. The Importance of Soft Skills

Some lawyers believe that they do not require any specific training in soft skills. They believe that, since they have become technically proficient in their area of expertise and are incredibly hard workers, they will be able to master soft skills with the same proficiency with which they are able to master their technical skills. Other lawyers believe that leadership and soft skills are qualities which by nature you either have or have not and that, if you are not born a leader or a great communicator, there is very little you can do to become one.

All of these beliefs are wrong and unjustified. A lawyer who denies the importance of soft skills will generally experience difficulties and setbacks in their career. Typically, they will struggle to develop their business by winning new clients and new instructions or, within their firm, struggle to manage their team by retaining and motivating their assistants and support staff.

How many times, for example, have you heard of a lawyer failing to secure instructions from a potential client because of a poor sales pitch despite the fact that they had the best credentials, capabilities and technical skills? Perhaps something in the way the lawyer communicated with the potential client did not give the client the confidence they needed to instruct that lawyer with their business. Even though the client may have known that the lawyer was the most skilled to undertake the job, they offered the job to someone else who appeared to possess some "intangible qualities" that the first lawyer did not possess.

Research suggests that only forty per cent. of a buying decision comes down to objective factors such as the suitability of the technical solution on offer and that the other sixty per cent. comes down to emotional factors such as the ability of the person pitching for the work to build personal rapport and trust with the buyer. Despite this, professionals, and especially lawyers, still believe that the best way to deliver a sales pitch is by pointing out their skills, capabilities and relevant experience rather than by trying to build a personal and special rapport with the potential client.

Similarly, how many times have you heard of a lawyer who failed to deliver good quality advice in a transaction or case due to bad project management? Things would have gone differently had the relevant project been managed and organised effectively from the very beginning.

Soft skills are also essential for every lawyer who wishes to become a partner in their firm. Often when existing partners consider an associate's potential for partnership, they will look at the associate's technical skills as well as their soft skills. The partners know that the associate can get the job done, but can they inspire others to do the same? The associate may have acquired excellent legal skills, but are they ready to take on all of the additional responsibilities that partnership gives such as generating and managing client relationships, supervising and training junior lawyers and handling firm management duties?

While the particular mix of soft skills required may vary from one firm to another and, within the same firm, from one practice area to another, every lawyer practising law today require to employ effective soft skills in their job.

3.   Soft Skills Training

The aim of this book is to provide an introduction to the soft skills most relevant to the legal profession and explore certain related areas.

Chapters 2 to 4 of this book deal with communication skills, namely non-verbal communication, verbal communication and business etiquette respectively. Among other things, these chapters introduce the concept of perception, a concept of utmost importance in communication, and look at the ways you can improve the perception others have of you by working on your image.

Chapter 5 deals with career management and provides practical suggestions on how to become partner in a law firm. Chapter 6 deals with business development. It contains advice on the topics of marketing and sales pitches, two topics that are often frowned upon and treated with fear or scepticism by lawyers. The remaining chapters 7 to 9 deal with delegation and project management, public speaking and time and stress management respectively.

This book does not purport to be a definitive guide on the topics covered but only to present the basic concepts and techniques that will enable you to employ soft skills more effectively in your work and, ultimately, help you become a better lawyer. If, after reading this book, you feel you may require further training in one or more of the areas covered, you may wish to seek additional specialised training by attending personal development seminars, management or business courses, or by contacting a professional coach. You may also wish to read some of the books, articles and publications that are listed in the bibliography and further reading section at the end of this book.

From now on you should take advantage of any available professional development programme offered by your firm and must be proactive in filling any gaps left in your knowledge following such programme. Ask yourself what resources your firm offers and what activities it organises that could provide you with an opportunity to develop the soft skills that you most require. From now on, soft skills should become an integral part of your training programme.

Although your professional plate is probably more than full with the practice of law and business development activities, it is a wise investment of your time to also focus on soft skills development. Developing soft skills should not only be a matter of professional development but also (and foremost) a matter of personal development and self-improvement. This has a number of profound implications, some of which will be explored later.

4.   A Proactive Approach to Training

If you wish to learn how to improve your soft skills, you have to take an active role in your learning process. You should identify by yourself the skills that you most need to develop and the specific activities that will help you develop those skills.

If you are a junior lawyer and would like to refine your leadership skills, for example, you may want to volunteer to take on voluminous assignments, like a sizeable due diligence or disclosure exercise, which would require you to delegate tasks to a number of people and coordinate and supervise the work done by others. You may also want to let your supervisor know that you wish to practise your leadership skills so that they will be able to provide an opportunity as soon as one arises. If the opportunity does not arise, try to do some voluntary work. You may acquire strong leadership and organisation skills by becoming involved in a trade association or helping your favourite charity.

If you are a slightly more senior lawyer and you wish to improve your public speaking skills, you may want to contribute to "introduction to practice" programs for more junior lawyers or trainees or deliver a presentation to your colleagues on a specific topic. These speaking opportunities will build your knowledge in the substantive areas concerned and expand your public speaking skills. They will also enhance your reputation and visibility within your firm which, as will be explained later, is crucial for career progression purposes.

If you are a newly appointed partner and would like to refine your business development skills, you may want to observe the partners in your firm who generate the most business and analyse the way they achieve that result. How do they market their services to the public at large? How do they make contacts with new clients? Which social or business networking events do they attend? Is their way to develop business different from the way you do it? Perhaps it may be time to emulate them and see if you generate the same results. Depending on your relationship with the partner in question, you could ask them to share their experience with you and give you some advice. Their support and feedback could be invaluable.

To conclude, there are a number of areas on which you will have to actively work from today if you wish to become a better lawyer. Acquiring training in soft skills is a process that will require ongoing effort and commitment from you. However, if you believe that you can improve and have faith in yourself and your capabilities, you will be able to take on board the techniques and skills taught in this book and gradually incorporate them into your daily practice.

You will then notice the difference these techniques and skills will make in your work and reap the rewards of all your efforts. You will notice that working will be easier and soon you will become more confident and more in control of your work. Remember, if you can get your soft skills right, you will be ahead of your colleagues and competitors, and up to the task in any situation.

CHAPTER 2 – NON-VERBAL COMMUNICATION

1. Introduction

This chapter deals with the topic of non-verbal communication. It looks at how you can improve the way you appear to the people who are around you. It contains a number of suggestions on how to improve your professional and personal image and draws your attention to a number of small things that can make a big difference in the way you are perceived by other people, within and outside your firm.

Among other things, this chapter looks at the way you dress, your business and casual wardrobe and how to avoid common mistakes, so far as casual dressing is concerned. It will then explain the importance of posture and body language and look at ways to maintain your posture always under control so that you can project a positive, confident and friendly image at all times.

2. How You Dress

Do not be tempted to downplay the truth in the old saying "before you speak a word, your clothes have already spoken volumes". Assumptions about your business ability are always made on the spot, sometimes based solely upon your appearance and how you dress. Your reputation may be negatively affected if your clients or the colleagues with whom you work form an unfavourable impression of how you dress. How you dress affects how the people around you perceive your ability to conduct business professionally.

Whilst the above may sound obvious, chances are you can remember at least a few occasions in which you found yourself noticing that someone with whom you work was dressed in a sloppy or inappropriate fashion. Or a few occasions where you did not dress at your best and felt uncomfortable because you should have dressed better.

Although there will be a number of occasions in which you may be tempted to downplay the importance of how you dress, do not give in to that temptation and always make a positive effort to dress the best that you can. The people you meet will take positive notice if you always dress properly irrespective of the circumstances.

Dress in professional attire and in principle conservatively. If you are starting a new job or have moved to a new country, observe how the other lawyers in your firm (especially the partners) dress for work and match their style. If you have had the chance to work in a number of different firms over your career, you will have noticed how dress codes and expectations vary considerably from one firm to the other. So what may appear as ordinary dress in one firm might be considered as over-dressing in another.

If you are a partner, exuding a positive, professional image by the clothes you wear will further support your credibility. It will, in addition, set the tone for your associates.

Therefore take the time to review your business wardrobe. The most common mischiefs to look for are worn out clothes (especially shirts) or clothes that require small repairs. Give away old clothes even if that means giving away a suit with which you "fought many battles". Get rid of old shoes that may have been left unused under your desk for many years now.

If you have not already done so, organise your wardrobe by separating the great outfits from those that you would wear on a daily basis. Keep all the components for both sets clean and ready to go at a moment's notice.

How well you dress and what colours you wear may also exercise an influence upon your mood on the day and your performance at work. You may have noticed that if one day you dress particularly smart you will feel happier and perform at your best.

Colours might influence your performance in many ways. Wear red if you wish to assert your authority because red can make you look and feel confident and in control. Avoid red, however, if you wish others to open up to you, since you risk intimidating them.

Wear green to help you concentrate - it will focus your attention on what needs to be done. Blue will calm you in times of stress, but avoid it if you want to be creative. Purple is a brain-booster according to marketing specialists, so wear purple when you need to be bursting with ideas. Black gets you taken seriously, but can make you conform to the corporate stereotype making it harder to stand out and potentially leading to the presumption you lack flair.

2.1   Casual Dressing

The purpose of casual dressing, as you may already know, is to increase morale and productivity in the office by removing some of the pressure of always having to look businesslike and formal.

The concept, born in the United States, has had a varying degree of success among law firms in recent years. Whilst certain firms have rejected the idea of casual dressing altogether, other firms have allowed casual dressing on Fridays, the summer months, the Christmas period, etc. and a few US firms have even instituted everyday casual dressing.

You can judge for yourself whether casual dressing does actually achieve its purpose. But, whatever your opinion on the topic, you should be careful as to what you wear on casual days since a lot is at stake here. People within your firm will gain an insight into (or make assumptions about) who you *really are* based on how you *appear* when you are not dressed formally.

How a person dresses on a casual day can indeed provide a lot of information about that person, including their social background, their values and their motivations.

It is invariably the case that, if you get to see someone in their ordinary clothes, you'll get to see them for who they really are and how they perceive themselves. Whilst you and your work colleagues might all look the same when dressed in a dark suit, you will not look the same when dressed in your ordinary clothes. In fact, stark differences are likely to show-up.

Some people believe that a person's choice of casual wear is one of those fine details that confirm the persistence of the class system (at least in matters of taste). It is no wonder therefore that the uniform of a suit at work is often desirable.

Make sure therefore that when you attend work on a casual day you do not forget the importance of how you appear. Depending on the circumstances, you may wish to take this opportunity to give your work colleagues a clear message about who you really are, your social background and your values. Or you may wish to take a more conservative approach and simply match your work colleagues' dress code.

Whatever your approach, observe carefully how your work colleagues dress and observe whatever dress policy has been promulgated by your firm. In case of doubt, err on the side of conservatism and always exercise judgment. For example, you should always wear hose or socks, a collared shirt, a belt and ensure that your shirt is always tucked in. Avoid in principle sleeveless blouses or shirts, barefoot sandals, open-toes shoes and open or unbuttoned shirts.

Especially if you are a junior lawyer, you should avoid wearing jeans and a t-shirt, irrespective of the weather, and even if fellow colleagues wear them. It is almost invariably the case that more senior lawyers will frown upon a junior lawyer wearing jeans and a t-shirt. Irrespective of your age, a hippy or, even worse, a shabby look is almost invariably frowned upon, directly at you or behind your back.

Similar considerations apply if you are a slightly more senior lawyer wishing to become a partner. If the partners do not dress casual on casual days (as sometimes happens), you should consider doing the same. Remember that how you dress on casual days will provide information about your social background. Depending on your circumstances and the people you work for, this might be used for or against you.

Lastly, you may consider dressing formally even on a weekend or casual day if you are meeting people from outside your firm (whether clients or other lawyers).

2.2   Dressing Finesse

Overcoat Etiquette

Proper etiquette requires you to remove your overcoat whenever you enter a building or office. Do not wait in a lounge or other waiting area with your overcoat still on.

Once removed, you may wish to carry your overcoat over the left arm. By doing this, your right hand will remain free and you will be able to shake hands with the person you are visiting without any awkward movements.

You may wish to check in your overcoat whenever someone asks you to do so, after having emptied the pockets of any valuable items. Always check in your overcoat at a restaurant if asked to do so.

Button Etiquette

Detailed rules apply so far as the buttoning of men suits is concerned. These rules vary depending on the style and the button placement of the suit.

A single-breasted suit should be kept buttoned while standing. In a three-button suit, the bottom button should never be fastened. If you want to have only one button done up, this should be the middle of the three buttons. If you want to have two buttons done up, you should button the middle and top buttons. For a two button suits it is appropriate to fasten the top button, but by no means the bottom button only. When seated, all buttons should be unbuttoned so as to preserve the line and tailoring of the suit.

Double-breasted suits should, by contrast, always be kept buttoned whether you are standing or seated. When there is more than one button, only the top button should be fastened. Often, this is the only one that can be properly fastened, because the bottom button lacks a corresponding interior flap. However, if you are wearing a six-button double-breasted suit (a type which was particularly popular in the 1980s), you should fasten the bottom button only.

"Lounge Suit"

When an invitation you receive contains the less common specification "Lounge suit", you should wear an outfit which falls somewhere in between "Black tie" and "Smart casual" (e.g. a jacket/blazer and a tie).

Men can wear their business suits without problems. Women can do the same, and perhaps add a smart accessory.

Striped Ties

If you are a foreigner visiting the UK, you may wish to avoid wearing striped ties since there is a risk that the stripe may "belong" to an institution such as a school, university, club or military regiment of which you are not a member and this may be a cause of embarrassment.

3. Meaning of Non-Verbal Communication

The expression non-verbal communication is used to indicate the messages an individual transmits, intentionally or unintentionally, through their facial expression, their posture, their gestures and the sound of their voice – its tone, pace, stress and intonation – when speaking to other people.

A number of experts in communication say that non-verbal communication is more important than verbal communication. According to psychologist Albert Mehrabian, for example, body language comprises 55% of the force of any response, whereas the verbal content only provides 7%, and "paralanguage", or the intonation, pauses and sighs given when answering, represents 38% of the emphasis.

In other words, it is not what a person says that matters, but how they say it. The actual words spoken have the least impact in communication, while non-verbal clues, including voice tone, facial expression and body movements, have the most.

Voice tone, for example, is particularly important and often prevails over spoken words when there is a conflict between the two. This happens, for instance, when someone tells you that they are not angry by yelling or that they are interested in what you are saying in an unconvincing tone.

Still, most professionals discount the importance of non-verbal communication because their education and training placed more emphasis on spoken words. Indeed, it is invariably the case that, when preparing for an important one-to-one conversation or group presentation, lawyers spend considerable time thinking carefully about the words that they are going to use (contents) and only give small consideration, if any, to the tone of voice they are going to use or what posture and gestures are going to accompany their speech (delivery).

Being able to master non-verbal communication can be a very precious professional tool. The ability to control and manage your body language and the non-verbal signals that you send, combined with the ability to read other people's body language and the non-verbal signals that you receive from them, can add to your effectiveness at work and enhance the quality of your communication whether you are communicating with a client, work colleague or team member.

Once you gain an understanding of non-verbal communication, you will be able to minimize the possibility of giving a false impression of yourself and learn to trust your gut instinct.

3.1 Body Language Basics

Body language is comprised of the non-verbal signals that your facial expression, your posture and your gestures convey to other people when you communicate with them.

13

You do not need to become a body language expert to get the most out of your body language, as long as you learn a few basic concepts and rules, which are introduced below. Whilst the following information is not exhaustive, it will certainly give you the basics to get you started, at least so far as managing your own body language is concerned.

Comfort Zones and Angles

Whenever you meet someone and start a conversation with them, observe the distance that you spontaneously create between your respective bodies and the angles at which your bodies stand to each other.

So far as distance is concerned, there are three main distances (sometimes called zones or territories) in body language: the business distance, the personal distance and the intimate distance.

The business distance is of approximately 1.5 meters to 1 meter. This is the space where you can comfortably talk to people you are doing business with.

The personal distance is of approximately 1 meter to 50 centimetres. This is the space where you can comfortably talk to people you know and trust, typically your friends and the work colleagues whom you have known for a long time.

The intimate distance is of approximately 50 cm or closer, and is the space for family members and loved ones.

Remember, however, that the above distances can vary significantly from one country to another.

In principle, when talking to someone, you should always keep the right distance, that is the distance that the relationship existing between you and that person dictates. As you will probably know, people become uncomfortable if their personal space, or preferred distance from others, is invaded. If you stand too close to the person you are talking to you risk irritating or even intimidating them. You may be marked as pushy or aggressive.

At the same time, however, if you stand or sit too far away from that person you may give the opposite impression of being cold and detached. Depending on the circumstances, the other person may even feel that you are not being sincere or shying away.

During your conversation, you may want to move from time to time closer to or further from the person you are talking to for a number of reasons. Whenever you do so, observe the other person's reaction.

If you wish to emphasize a key point of what you are saying, or if the other person seems generally sceptical or is losing its interest, you may want to move slightly closer and observe whether you have gained their full attention.

Likewise, if you wish to stress your sincerity or your confidence, you may want to lean slightly forward, look the person in the eye and perhaps accentuate your gestures. Remember that leaning back and looking down is generally interpreted as a lack of confidence.

By moving closer to the person you are talking to, you might also be able to get a feeling of how much that person is engaged in what you are saying, and thus gauge their interest. Broadly speaking, the more engaged in a conversation two persons are the closer they stand to each other.

If you move closer to the person you are talking to and they back away or even stay where they are, it is probable that that person is not particularly engaged in what you are saying and you should accordingly pull back a little since your movement might not have been welcome. By contrast, if you notice that they get closer as a response to your movement, chances are that that person is listening attentively and with interest to what you are saying.

So far as body angles are concerned, suffice it to say that if you keep you body straight in front of the other person's body you will convey a message of openness, sincerity and attention. By contrast, the more angle you create the more you will give the impression of being hiding something from the other person and not being sincere or simply not interested in what the other person is saying.

Remember this simple rule: people angle towards people they find attractive, friendly and interesting and angle away from those they don't.

Mirroring

Mirroring (also known as matching behaviour) is a powerful technique you can use to establish and maintain rapport with a person you have just met. It works essentially in one-to-one communication or small group situations, but not in group presentations.

In its simplest terms, when you meet someone and wish to engage them in conversation or otherwise establish rapport with them, you should observe their facial expression, posture and gestures and replicate (mirror) them in your own body language.

During the conversation, follow the other person's body movements, posture and gestures without being too obvious about it. This technique will help you to engage people in conversation and gain and maintain their interest for as long as you wish.

Congruence

As illustrated above, whenever there is conflict between the words that an individual uses and the non-verbal signals that they send when communicating with someone, the non-verbal signals (including body language signals) will often override what is being said. Consciously or unconsciously, people generally rely more on the non-verbal messages that they perceive rather than the words they hear.

It has been suggested that this phenomenon can be explained by an inborn belief that non-verbal signals are generally more eloquent, honest and accurate than spoken words. While words can deceive -

many people do not mean what they say or say what they mean - body language is more spontaneous and less controlled and therefore prone to show the true feelings and attitudes of a person.

When you are communicating with someone, you should therefore ensure that your body language is always in harmony with, and reinforces the meaning of, your spoken words.

Do not assume that if you believe in what you are saying and are not hiding anything to your listener, your body language will automatically back up the contents of your words. In fact, a lot of people fail to deliver any meaningful non-verbal message when they communicate.

Learn therefore to monitor your body language when you speak and use your body language to reinforce the meaning of your words. This way you will become a more powerful communicator.

The next time you wish to reassure a client that your suggested course of action is the most appropriate in the circumstances, try to accompany your verbal reassurances with a reassuring gesture like an open movement of the arm and a relaxed smile. If you will also speak at a slow pace and use a low-pitched and relaxed voice tone, chances are that your client will immediately feel reassured and follow your advice.

3.2   Positive Body Language

You should always ensure that your body language projects in every situation the image of a confident, approachable and friendly professional with an enthusiastic, positive and confident attitude.

The way you can achieve this is by adopting what communication experts call a "positive body language" (sometimes called "good body language"), that is a type of body language that can create a positive feeling about you. Positive body language is opposed to negative body language, which is comprised of those types of body language that project images of nervousness, lack of confidence or lack of interest.

The following paragraphs contain suggestions that will help you maintain positive body language in every situation.

General Appearance

You should ensure that your body language always reflects calmness and control.

If you feel nervous, you may wish to practise self-talk about being calm and be aware of controlling your gestures and posture. When you jiggle your foot, tap your fingers and crack your knuckles you display your nervousness or discomfort about the situation you are in.

Instead, try to breath deeply, sit or stand straight without slouching, and make eye contact with the people around you. People will think that you are calm and collected and, before long, you will actually be.

Keep always an engaging smile and a pleasant facial expression and learn to smile with your eyes as opposed to the whole face. This is a useful precaution because it's easy for someone to tell if you are trying too hard to smile.

As mentioned earlier in this book, smiling indicates that you are a friendly, open and approachable person. If you remain tight-lipped, you will send the message that you are either nervous or unreceptive, neither of which will help you establish a positive image.

So try to smile even if you do not feel like doing it or are not in the right mood. When you need a smile, relax your facial muscles and recall a pleasurable experience or a good friend. With practice, this will bring almost on demand that easy, encouraging smile that will help you establish rapport with your colleagues and clients and make you a better communicator.

With practice, you will also learn to alter your facial expression to match the message you wish to convey. You will learn to smile and maintain good eye contact when you are saying something friendly and wish to convey openness and honesty.

Whilst it is important to smile, it is however equally important not to overdo it. If, for example, you enter a meeting beaming broadly, the people in the meeting might wonder what you have to be so pleased about. So enter positively and confidently, be observant of the general atmosphere and mood and conform to those vibes.

Eye Contact

Eye contact is one of the most important aspects of dealing with people, especially people you have just met. Maintaining good eye contact shows respect and interest in what people have to say and give them a feeling of comfort and genuine warmth in your company.

If the eyes are the windows to the soul, then you must use them to allow others to see your sincerity, self-confidence and knowledge. Looking someone in the eye also puts you on an even footing with the person you are looking at.

If you avoid eye contact, you might appear as being uncomfortable or unsure of yourself or simply lacking interest in the people around you or their conversation.

Do not overdo eye contact, though. It has been observed that in the United Kingdom people tend to keep eye contact around 60-70% of the time. Doing it more than that can cause discomfort or anxiety in the person you are gazing or create tension between the two of you. You may also wish to avoid eye contact during long silences and avoid continuous eye contact, which may be taken as a sign of insincerity or even lying.

As an alternative to eyeball-to-eyeball gazing, you may wish to keep your gaze generally into the lower part of the face of the person you are talking to, that is just below their eyes. This is sometimes called "intimate gaze". Intimate gaze is perfectly friendly and less intimidating than full eye contact and particularly appropriate if you wish to use eye contact to underline an important point while talking.

Be careful, however, that you do not give the impression of deliberately avoiding eye contact. As mentioned, this might give the impression that you are being evasive, lack confidence or that you are simply not interested in the matter at hand.

If you are speaking at a meeting, do not try to maintain eye contact with everyone because your efforts might affect your ability to concentrate on what you are saying. It is perfectly acceptable to focus on the last person that spoke and make rapid eye contact with the other people from time to time.

Lastly, remember that, especially so far as eye contact is concerned, what is acceptable practice in the UK may not be acceptable elsewhere, particularly if you are dealing with people from non-Western countries. In Japan, for example, direct eye contact may be impolite and be interpreted as a sign of weakness or worse may indicate sexual overtones.

General Posture

Posture is the next thing you should learn to master. Get your posture right and you will automatically feel better. A good posture makes you feel good almost instantly. Next time you notice that you are feeling a bit down, take a look at how you are standing or sitting. Chances are you may be slouched over with your shoulders sagging down and inward. This may collapse your chest and inhibits good breathing, which in turn can make you feel nervous or uncomfortable.

The following practical suggestions will help you maintain a good body posture:

- When standing, stand straight with both feet on the floor and resist the temptation to lean or rest against a wall or table surface, even if you feel tired.

- Walk with grace and ease with your arms swinging and take determined strides. Do not drag or shuffle your feet when walking and avoid taking short or choppy strides.

- Hold your head level and keep your chin up. When you want to appear confident and self-assured keep your head level both horizontally and vertically. Conversely, when you want to be friendly and in the listening, receptive mode, tilt your head just a little to one side or other. You can shift the tilt from left to right at different points in the conversation.

- Arms give away the clues as to how open and receptive we are to everyone we meet and interact with, so keep your arms out to the side of your body or behind your back. In general terms the more outgoing you are as a person, the more you will tend to use your arms with big movements. The quieter you are the less you will move your arms away from your body. So, try to strike a natural balance and keep your arm movements midway. In order to come across in the best possible light, never cross your arms in front of others.

- Legs are the furthest point away from the brain, consequently they are the parts of the body that are hardest to control consciously. They tend to move around a lot more than normal when a person is nervous, stressed or being deceptive. So it is best to keep them as still as possible in most situations, especially at work meetings. Be careful too in the way you cross your legs.

- At a meeting, sit straight on your chair without slouching and keep your hands on the table. You may wish to rest your forearms on the table with your hands lightly clasped. This will put you in a perfect position to gesture if needed. Whenever you wish to show attention, lean slightly forward towards the person who is speaking. This will make you look more involved in the conversation.

Hand Gestures

Your hands should always follow naturally, and move in symphony with, the contents of your conversation. They should flow naturally and match the tone of the conversation and the degree of animation of the participants. Put energy into your gestures but don't be over-animated.

In principle, you should keep your gestures to a minimum and use them intentionally only when you wish to emphasize a point or key message or to signal that you are being sincere. Try to make ample and regular movements with your hands and keep your palms slightly up and outward to show friendliness and sincerity. Let you hand movements be seen and let them flow naturally.

When you are talking to someone, keep both hands where they can be seen. Whilst nobody is afraid you are going to brandish a blade and try to stab them, hidden hands are sometimes still perceived as a sign of lack of sincerity. You might give the impression that you are concealing something. Avoid therefore keeping your hands in your pockets, behind your back or, if you are seated at a meeting, under the meeting table.

Likewise, you may wish to avoid palm down gestures, which are generally seen as dominant, emphasizing and possibly aggressive, especially when there is no movement or bending between the wrist and the forearm.

You may also wish to avoid crossing your arms, especially if you are at a meeting with a client or colleague that you have just met. Crossing arms (or legs) may look casual and should therefore be avoided unless the person you are with takes the lead, in which case mirroring them could help you establish rapport.

Guard against using gestures that may betray your nervousness such as clenching or wringing your hands, holding your legs or arms tensely or playing with a watch or ring, and generally any wild or anxious gesticulation. All these gestures will simply attract attention to your hands rather than the content of your speech and therefore distract your audience from what you are saying. If you find yourself making any of those gestures, just stop. This is particularly important when you are delivering a public presentation.

Handshake

As a professional, you should always shake hands when you are introduced to someone and state clearly your name and position unless an introducer has done that for you. When entering a meeting, you may wish to consider whether it is appropriate to shake hands with all the participants or only the people sitting next to you (and perhaps nod to the other people you know at the meeting). When meeting someone for the first time, if they don't offer their hand first, offer yours. It's a sign of confidence.

There is no need to stress the importance of a good handshake. Conventional wisdom has it that you can learn a lot about a person from their handshake but this is not necessarily the case. This said, it is probably true that a poor handshake does generally create a feeling of dislike (who does not dislike a boneless hand extended as though it were a spray of sea-weed?) to the other person and that getting your handshake right will help you to make a positive first impression.

A proper handshake is made briefly but you should try to convey a feeling of strength and warmth in your clasp. One good pump and a concise greeting (such as "I'm delighted to meet you") combined with solid eye contact will do.

When shaking hands, keep extending your hand until you hook thumbs. Try this and you'll see how it works and then practise it until it comes naturally. Take the other person's hand fully at the palm and not by the fingers.

It can be a good idea to hold on to the person's hand for a moment longer than you would do naturally, literally holding the other person's attention while the opening pleasantries are exchanged.

If you sweat easily, make sure that your palm is dry by discreetly wiping it before you shake hands.

So far as strength is concerned, you should again find the right balance between a bone crushing and a limp handshake to suit your personality and the situation. Generally speaking, a too firm handshake will make you appear aggressive and make the other person want to keep you at a distance once they know you use it. They might even think that you are doing it deliberately to give the impression of a dominance you don't actually possess. At the same time, a weak handshake will make you appear passive and weak.

Depending on the situation, you may want to convey a sense of sincerity or warmth. This may be the case when meeting someone in person for the first time after having spoken to them over the phone a number of times. To do this, loosen the grip just a bit and briefly place your left hand on top of the person's right hand as it shakes yours. Again, practise this until it comes naturally.

Be wary of appearing too warm though. Grasping someone else's forearm or shoulder with your free hand as you shake will almost certainly make them think that you are insincere. You should also avoid the so-called "dominant handshake", which is a palm down handshake where you let the other person clasp your fingers only. This kind of handshake gives the other person an immediate sense of unfriendliness.

Showing Confidence

The following are practical suggestions that may help you to appear more confident in front of your colleagues, clients or superiors. These suggestions will help you convey the image of being a confident person and will be particularly useful if you are a trainee or a junior assistant working in a large firm.

- Whenever a partner is expecting to see you in their office, enter their office politely but with the confidence of someone who is being awaited. Without being impolite, try to avoid knocking on the door, or opening it and peeking in, since these behaviours show hesitation. If, when you get to the partner's office, the partner is no longer able to see you, they will certainly let you know politely.

- If the partner you are seeing receives a phone call when you are in their office, start pretending to review any papers you may have in front of you so that you can give them a sense of privacy. Don't show annoyance or impatience about the interruption or offer to leave the office. Once again, if the partner anticipates that it will be a long call, they will politely ask you to come back later.

- Whenever you are attending a meeting with other members of your team, if possible, sit next to the most influential and senior member (most likely a partner). For some unknown reason, a person's authority permeates those around them and you could benefit from this. Sitting next to the most influential and senior team member will also convey the message that you are not afraid of power.

- Lastly, don't be afraid to sit at the head of a long or oval table. From the head of the table, you can see everyone in the room and, just as importantly, everyone can see you.

3.3   Negative Body Language

Negative types of body language all send the same negative message, that is, that you are nervous, lack confidence, are impatient or uninterested, etc.   Listed below are the most common types of negative body language, together with an indication of the impression that they generally give to other people.

- Jiggling the content of your pockets, clearing your throat, biting a pen or other object, fidgeting your hands or running your fingers though your hair. These behaviours will all be interpreted as a sign of nervousness and are generally accompanied by the building-up of anxiety or worry.

- Keeping your chin down, making a tight-lipped grin, frowning, squinting, touching your nose or face, darting eye movements, pointing with your fingers, rubbing the back of your neck or chopping one hand into palm of the other. These behaviours all show insecurity.

- Keeping tightly crossed arms, high on the chest. This gives the impression that you are defensive and uninterested.
- Speaking in a high-pitched, fast-paced voice. You will sound girly and lacking authority.

- Rolling on your heels. This will make you appear childish.
- Lazing about on a chair. This will make you appear arrogant and lazy.
- Shrugging your shoulders. This will signal that you don't believe what has been said, even if it was you who said that.
- Touching your face. This will be interpreted as a sign of nervousness or possibly even dishonesty.
- Stroking your neck. This may make you seem stressed or flirtatious.
- Foot tapping. This will show impatience.
- Pen drumming. This will show boredom.

3.4   Masquerading

The expression masquerading is used in body language terminology to indicate the behaviour of those people who emphasise excessively their body language in an attempt to appear all too important, confident and assertive.

You may have met people like that before. They "stand tall" in a far too stiff upright posture or try to "tower" you when you engage them in conversation. They appear over-confident, self-important and arrogant.

Most of the times these people are using their body language to appear more important, authoritative or confident than they really are. They are, in other words, intentionally pretending or faking qualities that they do not possess. Their excessive emphasis, however, accompanied by a lack of spontaneity, will make this obvious and leave the people around them with a very negative impression.

Sometimes, however, people who are inexperienced at managing their body language (because, for example, they have just become aware of the importance of body language), commit the mistake of over-emphasising their body language and overdo most of their newly adopted postures and gestures.

These people, in a genuine effort to appear more confident and friendly, unintentionally end up giving other people a negative impression.

Try to avoid this common mistake and, especially if you are new to the concept of body language, monitor constantly your posture and gestures to ensure that you do not put excessive emphasis in them. Over time, things will become more natural and you will soon reap the benefits that adopting a positive body language will provide.

3.5   Videoconferencing

Before moving on to the next chapter, which will deal with verbal communication, it may be useful to provide you with one last suggestion so far as body language is concerned.

Whenever you are attending a videoconference, keep all your body movement to a minimum, since video communication will magnify every gesture and movement you make. Try to avoid making expansive gestures with your arms or hands, marked facial expressions and, needless to say, avoid slouching, looking around, rubbing your nose, pulling your ear, etc.

CHAPTER 3 – VERBAL COMMUNICATION

1. Introduction

This chapter contains suggestions aimed at improving your verbal communication. It contains suggestions as to how you can communicate more effectively when you speak to your clients and colleagues and practical tips on how you can improve your ability to engage in small conversation with people, in particular people you have just met, for example, at a conference or networking event.

2. How You Sound: Your Voice Tone

As mentioned earlier in this book, how you say something is often more meaningful than what you say. How you sound does not refer to the content of your message but rather to your tone of voice, speed of speech and the volume, rhythm, pitch, breathiness and resonance of your voice.

How you sound contributes to the impression you give people when you speak. Remember, combined with how you look, how you sound comprises more than 90 per cent of the perception of your credibility.

Voice tone is particularly important and you should always keep it under control. You should learn how to modulate your tone of voice when you speak, so that you can speak with the voice tone that is most appropriate to the message you wish to communicate, its recipient and all other circumstances.

If you are new to this concept, you might find the idea of modulating your tone of voice a little bizarre but, once you will have experienced how getting the voice tone right can improve your ability to communicate more effectively, you will never again engage in conversation before having positively considered what voice tone you are going to use.

It is not just actors and radio presenters who require this kind of training. If the sound of your own voice on your voicemail greeting leaves you puzzled (or ashamed), it is time that you learn how to modulate your voice.

The good news is that the way to do it could not be simpler: just experiment with your voice. Practise your speaking to develop variety in pace, modulation and pitch and do not stop until you have identified at least three difference tones, one low-pitched, one high-pitched and one in-between (neutral). A choice of three tones will be sufficient to give you enough tones to choose from in every situation.

You may use the neutral tone of voice as your default option. This should become your natural tone, the tone you will use whenever you engage in conversation unless you intentionally wish to adopt either of the other two tones. Your neutral tone should sound relaxed, warm and well modulated while at the same time being able to express enthusiasm and interest where appropriate. It should always convey courtesy and respect.

You may wish to use the high-pitched tone whenever you are engaged in a casual conversation and you wish to appear friendly and unpretentious. This tone, it has been suggested, should be used essentially outside work situations, when you are talking to your friends and family.

The low-pitched tone, as you might imagine, will be your first choice whenever you wish to convey a feeling of reassurance and express your confidence to someone, for example, a client. Remember to pronounce your words slowly and maintain a positive and confident body language throughout.

Once you have learned how to modulate your voice, you will be able to adopt the voice tone that is most appropriate to the message you wish to communicate in every situation and you will notice how your ability to communicate effectively will dramatically improve.

You will thus become a more powerful communicator and you will never again find yourself speaking in a weak, soft, hesitant or tremulous voice in any situation.

3. What You Say: Communicating Clearly

You may have heard before that communication should be as clear as possible. The following suggestions will hopefully help you achieve a clear communication.

- Give your bottom line first. Short sounds confident. Work out in advance what you really want to say and then say it clearly and directly, with no extra frills. This applies whether you are giving instructions to a colleague or advice to a client. Sound as though you know what you want or what you think, and people will believe you and know where they stand with you.

- Be clear and direct. Don't dilute your message, that is don't be wishy-washy about what you are saying or asking for. Too often people apologise, make excuses or give long explanations so that their listeners are given a very mixed message. Give your opinions in clear and certain terms, directly and without qualifiers unless really pertinent. Never say things like: "I'm sorry to have to ask you this", "I feel awful about this, but..." or "I wouldn't ask, only..."

- Use few words. The fewer the words you use, the bigger the impact. Powerful, effective people are always succinct. It's a good rule of thumb to make sure that you listen more often than you speak.

The above tips apply also to written communication.

4. Speaking on the Telephone

When speaking over the telephone it is particularly important to focus on your tone of voice and word choice. Without body language, you must rely primarily on your words and voice to communicate your ideas. In particular, ensure that your voice tone conveys courtesy and respect to your listeners and that your voice is pleasant.

Once again, assumptions about you, your professionalism and your ability to deliver what you promise will be made based on your voice and your words and how well you articulate and express your thoughts. The way you speak will impact the way you will be perceived. People will "hear" your personality and mannerisms through the tone of your voice and the words you use.

A small tip: when speaking on the telephone, remember to smile. If you have never tried this, you will be surprised of the effect smiling will have on the other person on the phone. Your smile will be "heard" in your voice and distinctively perceived. As a consequence, it will immediately turn the other person into a cooperative and positive attitude whatever the subject matter of the call.

The reason for this is that when you smile and change your facial expressions, you also alter the sound of your voice. Your vocal tone is greatly influenced by the manner you use your facial muscles.
In fact, if you have ever worked in telesales (perhaps when you were a student?), you may have learned that one of the oldest telephone sales tricks is to have a mirror near the telephone so you can monitor your facial expression throughout the call and be sure you are smiling all the time.

As a sign of respect to the other person, when you are on the phone you may wish to focus all your attention on the call and the person you are speaking with. Minimise any background noise and, more importantly, don't try to do things like typing on your keyboard, open your mail or talk or make gestures to someone in the room with you. Don't eat or drink while you are on the phone. The impression you will leave on your listeners will not be a good one.

Also, even if the call or the caller is extremely boring, don't pull faces to them! They will notice it immediately because any change in your facial expression will result in a change in your voice tone.

Lastly, whenever you leave a message, is always proper etiquette to leave your phone number even if you know the other person already has it. Your thoughtfulness will save them the time and effort of looking up your number. Ideally, you may wish to give your phone number twice when leaving a message, once at the beginning of the message and again in the end.

5.   Speaking at a Meeting

There is one single truth you should bear in mind when you attend a meeting: the sooner you speak at the meeting and the more you speak, the more credible you will appear to the people attending the meeting.

Whether you like it or not, if you do not speak early at a meeting, you will probably give the impression of not being actively participating or that you lack importance. When you attend a meeting, you should try therefore to be among the first two or three people to speak and to speak every ten to fifteen minutes thereafter, even just to show that you are actively participating.

For these purposes, you don't always have to say anything particularly meaningful. In fact, how many times have you attended meetings where you had very little, if anything, to contribute? Whatever the circumstances, remember to speak early and often in order to show participation and interest on your part.

If you don't have anything particularly meaningful to say, you may simply show support to what someone else, perhaps your client, is saying or ask a legitimate question or make a comment on an emerging theme. These are all equally good ways to make your presence known.

Don't overdo it though. Speaking early and often in a meeting should not be confused with being pushy or domineering and you do not want to appear as if you like the sound of your own voice.

6.   How to make conversation

Making conversation is a skill that can be acquired and improved. Even if you are not naturally talented, the art of making conversation is something that you can acquire and cultivate. Whilst it is probably true that conversing is easier for some people than for others, practice and a few suggestions will certainly help you to master the art if it does not come naturally to you.

In this chapter reference is mainly made to the conversations you have with your clients, colleagues, counterparties, etc, but a special emphasis is also placed on the so-called social conversations, that is the conversations that occur in a social context when you entertain existing or potential clients or engage in conversation with someone you have just met.

The suggestions contained in this chapter will hopefully build up your confidence, help you avoid the most common mistakes people make in conversation and help you become an even more pleasant and interesting person.

6.1 Become a better conversationalist

In order to become a better conversationalist, you have first to get rid of any shyness you might still feel when meeting new people or when you find yourself on your own in a social or networking context (that is, a room full of strangers).

Apart from any psychological consideration, if you feel you need to build up your confidence, you may find it useful to start conversing with everyone you encounter in your daily routine, like cashiers, waiters, people you are in a queue with, your neighbours, etc.

In particular, try to chat with people unlike yourself, from the elderly to teenagers to tourists to people from a social background different from yours. You will soon discover how easy it is to get rid of that slick image that too often is associated with lawyers.

Force yourself to get into every possible small-talk situation and you will soon acquire the confidence you need to become a better conversationalist. A daily dose of a few words of small talk will help you overcome any residual shyness you might still have.

After having acquired the confidence you need, you then have to become an "interesting person". Generally speaking, there are only two ways to be one.

The first is to be a genuinely interesting person. This is someone who cultivates many interests, plays sport, reads about everything, travels a lot and immerses themselves in culture, both high and low.

If you are a genuinely interesting person, you will automatically be an interesting conversationalist. Your knowledge and love for life will transpire in every word you say and you will never run out of conversational topics.

There is, however, a second way to be an interesting conversationalist, a way you could follow if, for whatever reason, you do not have many genuine interests, are not into sport, do not read too much, do not travel much, and, in summary, live a quieter and reserved family life.

If this is you, you can still become an exceptionally interesting conversationalist by learning the few tips and well-known (but too often forgotten) secrets that are presented in the following paragraphs.

6.2 Conversation topics

When you are about to attend a social gathering or other networking event, you should do some small talk preparation and prepare a few interesting conversation topics that will keep you conversing for as long as necessary.

Spend five to ten minutes reading a daily newspaper or a weekly magazine. Look for interesting articles in the following sections: current events, lifestyle, books and films, business and sport. Read the headlines and skim through a paragraph or two of the articles that you believe would be most suitable to discuss with the people that you will meet at the event.

Having some comments on a few current subjects will be an excellent way to get a conversation going and you will immediately *appear* a very knowledgeable and interesting conversationalist to the people you will be talking to. Even if you have not been to the latest painting exhibition, you can still appear knowledgeable and interesting as long as you know about that exhibition and can discuss it.

Of course, you will have to choose your topics carefully and be aware of which topics you should avoid in a social situation. The following topics, for example, are best avoided:

- Religion
- Politics
- Diet and health
- Personal philosophy
- Spouses (except in general terms)
- Ethnic background (remember that you should never make any assumption about a person's background, nationality or origins based on their look)
- Gossip
- Criticism

Other topics should also be avoided in certain situations. For example, if you are a foreigner visiting the UK you should avoid also the following topics:

- The European Union, Brussels and the Euro
- Northern Ireland
- The monarchy and the Royal Family
- Class and the class system
- Religion (especially if you are in Northern Ireland, Glasgow or Liverpool)
- Race and immigration
- Sex (and in particular homosexuality)

The following topics of conversation, by contrast, are generally welcomed:

- The weather (always a safe starting point!)
- Current affairs
- Light business topics (recent trends in the market, etc.)
- Culture, literature, art, and popular music
- Sport (in particular football)
- Animals
- Travel

If you are a foreigner visiting the UK, you may find that the following topics are also welcomed:

- British history
- Your immediate surroundings and positive experiences in the UK
- How good the food is (things have changed in recent years!)
- Real ale (i.e. traditional British beer)

6.3   *Interesting* Conversation topics

If you wish to talk about *interesting* conversation topics, you should first and foremost realise that *interesting* conversation topics are not generally the topics that interest you but those that interest the person you are talking to.

When you are engaged in conversation with someone, your focus and entire attention should be on the other person and their interests (and not yours). If you wish to appear as an interesting conversationalist, your conversation should cater for the interests of the person(s) you are talking to.

Sometimes, depending on the situation, it will be relatively simple to guess what topics the other person may wish to talk about and, if you have done your preparation beforehand, your conversation will run smoothly throughout.

By contrast, when you do not have a clue as to what might interest to the person you are talking to, your best bet will generally be to start "fishing" for topics. This means to start offering topics until the person you are talking to reveals their interest for one of them.

Keep in mind the list of welcome topics of conversation set out earlier. You should start, for example, by asking the other person about their vacations, movies they have seen recently, any books they may have read recently whether they follow any of the local sport teams or, in a more business oriented context, whether they have noticed any recent trends in the business market. It is always advisable to try to initiate conversation with open questions rather than an assertion of a personal point of view.

If the circumstances so permit, take the time to positively think about what might be interesting to the other person and the things that you think will be agreeable to your hearer. If you think, you will find a topic and a manner of presenting your topic that will interest and please the other person.

At a more sophisticated level, you might even want to take a sociological approach. You could observe the other person's age, sex, profession, likely social background and family status and take a view as to what their interests might be. You can then suggest, from the very beginning of the conversation, a topic that is more likely to interest that kind of person without the need to go fishing first.

If you closely monitor the other person's body language and facial expression, you will be in the best position to notice when you have found a topic that genuinely stimulates the other person's attention. Typically, you will notice a sudden reaction, an unexpected glance or shift to a more upright posture. Pupil dilatation will be the most powerful signal, if you are able the read it and the circumstances so permit.

Once you are confident you have found a topic of conversation that interests the person you are talking to, you can relax and enjoy your conversation. But remember, stick to that topic and do not change unless the other person does it first. Once again, if you wish to appear as an interesting conversationalist, your conversation should cater for the interests of the person(s) you are talking to and not yours.

6.4   Think before you speak

When the conversation is flowing, you may start enjoying yourself but don't let yourself go too much if you know, from past experiences perhaps, that you might commit a blunder by saying something inappropriate. You should always be considerate and think about what you say and to whom you say it.

Since nearly all the faults or mistakes in conversation are caused by not thinking enough, let your mantra be: "Think before you speak".

Make an effort to say only things that will be agreeable to the person you are talking to and keep your true thoughts and feelings to yourself if needs be. Remember that the purpose of your conversation is to have a pleasant time and not arguing or exchanging opinions about topics. Therefore, whatever your true thoughts and feelings might be, don't ever tell anyone your opinions if the other person might disagree with you or commence an argument.

Being agreeable also means being positive about everything and not focussing on ills, misfortune, or other unpleasant things. It also means not criticising anything or anyone whatever the circumstances and being free from judgment. For example, don't talk about the unattractiveness of a certain industry or occupation since you don't know whether the person you are talking to has, for example, a close relative working in that industry or engaged in that occupation.

If you stick to this conservative approach, you will sometimes appear as being too polite and politically correct but, generally speaking, this will be better than risking committing a blunder. At least you will not get it wrong.

7.   Active Listening

Another powerful way to be an interesting conversationalist is to be an interested and attentive listener. It may sound like a paradox, but nothing will be of greater help in making you appear as an interesting person than being a good listener.

When you are talking to other people, it is not so much what you say but how attentively you listen to what others have to say that will make you come across as an exceptionally interesting conversationalist.

Bear this in mind when you engage in conversation with someone at a social or networking event, especially if you did not have the time to prepare a few conversation topics beforehand.

Being an attentive listener, as opposed to an active talker, will also help you avoid talking imprudently and committing blunders. You may have heard before that "regrets are seldom for what you left unsaid" and that "the faults of commission are far more serious than those of omission".

Do not make the mistake of believing that the more you are able to talk, the more you will come across as brilliant conversationalists and will impress the people that you are talking to. In fact, you will just appear as being as a pest or a bore.

That is why someone who is able to listen to what others have to say and show genuine interest will be greatly appreciated and come across as a pleasant person worth having a conversation with. Interested and attentive listeners are a rare breed nowadays and are always valued and respected.

It has also been suggested that the reason someone who keeps silent except when they have something worthwhile to say often comes across as the most interesting person. This is because the person who keeps silent cannot have their depth plumbed whilst a chatterer will typically reveal every corner of their shallow mind in a few seconds.

Whenever conversing with someone, practise active listening. Be attentive as to what other people tells you and show genuine interest for what they say, their feelings and concerns.

Give the person who is talking your spontaneous and undivided attention and show your empathy where appropriate. Ask pertinent questions where necessary. People like to talk about themselves and their activities. Listen, laugh and smile often and make sure that your body language and gestures encourage those you are speaking with to relax and participate.

Give compliments where appropriate and, when making compliments, be sincere. Be cautious about giving compliments to everyone all the time but remember that giving compliments is part of good conversation.

The importance of empathy cannot be overemphasised, especially when discussing business with existing or potential clients. All too often busy lawyers are prone to treating a query from a client like a technical issue and fail to remember that behind any technical issue there is a person emotionally concerned with that issue and often worried by it. Empathizing with that person will help build a stronger relationship with your client and make the whole client-lawyer experience more human.

8.   Other Practical Suggestions

Don't Interrupt

Whenever someone is talking to you, don't ever interrupt them unless you wish to show your interest and reassure the person who is talking that you are listening attentively. Your brain can think many times faster than your mouth can speak but that is not a good reason to interrupt someone. It may feel natural to start talking before someone else has finished but you probably know how bad it can feel when someone does it to you. Not to interrupt someone is particularly important when negotiating a deal or if you wish to persuade someone to your way of thinking.

Avoid Argument

Be careful not to let an amiable conversation turn into a discussion. As mentioned earlier, if you disagree with what someone is saying, the best course of action you can take is to take no action at all and keep your thoughts to yourself. Otherwise you will just drag the conversation into contradiction and argument.

Depending on the circumstances, you may wish to say with a quiet and tactful tone of voice (remember the importance of voice tone) "I don't think I agree with you" and leave it there, if possible switching to another subject for a more enjoyable conversation. Don't ever try to persuade the other person that you are right and they are wrong because, even if you win that argument, you will certainly lose that person's goodwill.

Don't Be Too Clever

Remember the old saying "don't be too clever if you wish to be popular". The cleverest person is the one who makes the other person seem clever.

Don't Pretend

Don't pretend to be important. Don't pretend to be busy. Don't pretend to be sought-after. You will merely turn people (and potential clients) off.

Don't pretend to know more than you do when engaged in conversation on a topic you are not familiar with. To give your opinion on a topic you are not familiar with will just make you appear superficial. Only the very small mind hesitates to say "I don't know."

The Gift of Humour

The joy of joys is the person of light but unmalicious humour. People will be irresistibly attracted to you if you are able to make them laugh sincerely and they will love you for that.

And if you can show that you do not take yourself and life too seriously, you will do great things in conversation and, more generally, in life.

CHAPTER 4 – BUSINESS ETIQUETTE

1. Introduction

As a well-educated lawyer, you probably do not require any training in etiquette and good manners, at least so far as the basic rules of etiquette are concerned. During the years spent in education, law school and the training contract you will have certainly acquired a good knowledge of etiquette and good manners.

This chapter, therefore, will not spend any time teaching the basics of etiquette and will instead focus on a few, so to say, more "sophisticated", "advanced" or less known aspects of business etiquette and protocol. This chapter will try to explore certain grey areas of business etiquette and shed some light on how you are expected to behave in those situations where it is not easy to guess how proper etiquette expects you to behave.

Hopefully you will find this chapter interesting and will start to incorporate the suggestions presented in the following pages in your daily work.

In effect, the importance of maintaining a polished and professional appearance in every situation cannot be overemphasised. As mentioned earlier in this book, people are constantly observing your behaviour and appearance and making assumptions about your professional capabilities based on what they see.

It is particularly important, therefore, to be able to show a good knowledge and understanding of the rules of proper etiquette.

Knowing what to do in every situation will give you the confidence to behave with competence and elegance whatever the circumstances. You will appear knowledgeable, confident and in control and that will greatly enhance the way people will perceive you and the assumptions they will make about your professional capabilities.

Your clients, especially if they come from the highest social backgrounds, will pay particular attention to how you behave and measure you not only on the basis of your ability as a lawyer but also on your ability to abide by the rules of proper etiquette in every situation.

In fact, you may have noticed how certain clients give more importance to your knowledge of etiquette and good manners than your ability to deal with technical queries effectively. Your ability to impress these clients with your fine behaviour and exquisite manners will therefore be crucial.

Being able to display an in-depth knowledge of business etiquette and protocol will also make a big difference in the way you will appear to your work colleagues and superiors, and this will be crucial for you especially if you are a junior assistant working in a large firm.

Your ability to impress your colleagues and superiors with your manners will help you stand out from the crowd and enhance your career prospects. It has been said that manners can open doors that the best education cannot and this is especially true so far as lawyers (and professionals in general) are concerned.

Get your manners right and your career will greatly benefit.

2. Flexibility

Before starting to explore the topics dealt with in this chapter, it is important to highlight that the rules of etiquette will be particularly valuable for you if you are able to apply them with the required flexibility and good judgment. Flexibility and good judgment mean, in this context, that in any situation you should adjust your behaviour based on the people around you.

You should always try to match the behaviour and the expectations of the people around you and fine-tune yourself accordingly. The rules of etiquette are not strict rules and do not need to be followed to the letter in every situation. By contrast, they are flexible rules that must be adjusted depending on the circumstances.

If you fail to adjust yourself to match the behaviour and expectations of the people around you, you risk finding yourself out of place sometimes and unable to establish rapport with the people you are with, whether they are clients or work colleagues.

If you are dealing with individuals who have a laid back attitude, for example, you should adopt a relaxed and laid back attitude too and avoid behaving in a stiff, formal or polished fashion with them. Remember the concept of mirroring and Saint Ambrose's dictum "when in Rome do as the Romans do".

3.   Formal Introductions

There is no need to highlight the importance of being able to make introductions with style and elegance. Introductions have never fallen out of fashion and are still the foundation of any business dealing. You should therefore know how to make proper introductions and, if you do not already know how to do it, the following paragraphs will hopefully teach you how to do that, particularly with reference to third-party introductions (that is, how to introduce someone to another person or group of persons) and self-introductions (that is, how to introduce yourself to another person that you do not know).

Especially so far as third-party introductions are concerned, you will need to practise a lot before being able to introduce people properly. Don't be afraid however to make mistakes because, as you may have noticed, even when you fail to introduce people properly, the persons being introduced will still appreciate your efforts and be grateful to you for having made the introduction. There is nothing worse than failing to make an introduction when you should have done.

3.1   Third-Party Introduction

The purpose of a third-party introduction is to give two or more persons the opportunity to meet each other formally and start a conversation together. As the person who makes the introduction, you are responsible for ensuring that the introduction runs smoothly and is made in accordance with proper etiquette.

Introductions still retain a certain level of formality today so it is particularly important that you know the rules governing this topic.

When to make an introduction

The rules of etiquette determining when an introduction should be made, or not made, are not very well defined. In most situations, therefore, it will be for you to determine whether an introduction is appropriate or not.

It is sometimes suggested that you should not make unnecessary introductions but the meaning of this is open to interpretation. As a rule of thumb, you should consider whether the individuals concerned would be interested to be introduced to each other and whether there is sufficient time for them to converse together following the introduction.
Certainly, if the individuals concerned start talking to each other without a prior introduction, you should make a formal introduction as soon as possible.

Likewise, if you are having a group conversation and someone you know approaches you, you should immediately introduce the newcomer to the other persons in the group.

In both cases try to make the introduction without delay since the individuals concerned might feel slightly uncomfortable in talking to each other without having been properly introduced.

Who is introduced to whom

Determining who should be introduced to whom is one of the most difficult decisions that you will have to reach when making an introduction. The fact that you often have to decide on the spot and in a fraction of seconds will only make things more difficult.

In the business world, the younger of age/more junior person is introduced to the older of age/more senior person. Knowing the office seniority and company title of the individuals concerned will therefore be crucial. Certain people believe that office seniority is more important than age but this is questionable.

In addition, at least in a social setting, you should always introduce a gentleman to a lady, and never vice versa. Gender, by contrast, is irrelevant in a business context.

Introduction formulas

In the simplest form of introduction commonly used, simply mention the name of the more important person, pause, and then mention the name of the person being introduced.
"Mr Senior, Mr Junior"

This is another circumstance in which your tone of voice will be particularly important, you should accentuate the more important person's name to make it clear that you are introducing the less important person to them.

You should pronounce the more important person's name with a slightly rising inflection and the second name as a sort of mere statement of fact. Like in: "Are you there?" and "Yes I am."
"Mr Senior?" "Mr Junior."

Do not repeat "Mr. Senior? Mr Junior. Mr Junior? Mr Senior." Saying the names only once will be sufficient.

Once you have mastered this simplest form of introduction, you can then start practicing alternative and more sophisticated forms like the following:

"Mr Senior, I would like to introduce Mr Junior"
"Mr Senior, I would like to present Mr Junior" (the word "present" is preferable on more formal occasions to the word "introduce")
"Mr Senior, may I present/introduce Mr Junior?"
"Mr Senior, do you know Mr Junior?"
"Mr Senior, have you met Mr Junior?"

Speak slowly and clearly so that each name can be heard distinctively and always give the persons' full name (first and last).

Very few people in polite society are introduced by their formal titles but you should use a title such as Dr for those holding a PhD when you know the person concerned like their title to be used. You should use titles also when introducing a doctor, a judge or a bishop.

Once you have mastered all of the above forms of introduction, you can then start practicing more content-rich introductions. After having pronounced the two names, give an explanation of who the two persons are and perhaps add further information that might be used as a conversation opener by the persons concerned.

"Mr Senior, may I introduce Mr Junior, a new member of the corporate department at our firm. Mr Senior is general counsel of Corporation plc. Mr Junior recently completed his LLM in corporate finance at the University of Life. Mr Junior, as you probably know Corporation plc is one of the most prestigious clients of our firm. They are a leading player in the money-laundering industry."

Be very careful when you give an explanation of who the persons are since if you get it wrong you might offend the persons concerned or, if you give wrong information, reveal that you actually do not know much about the persons you are introducing.

3.2   Self-Introduction

You make a self-introduction every time you introduce yourself to another person or, having been introduced by someone else, you let the person to whom you have just been introduced know something more about yourself such as what kind of law you practise and the services your firm offers. Look at a self-introduction as an opportunity to promote yourself briefly.

When to make a self-introduction

As a rule of thumb, you should make a self-introduction every time you feel that the person standing or sitting next to you would feel more comfortable after you have introduced yourself and explained who you are and what you do. Helping people feel comfortable in every situation is an important part of good etiquette.

The most common circumstance in which you should take the initiative and introduce yourself is when you are sitting at a meeting or a meal next to someone to whom you have not been introduced. A self-introduction is warranted in such circumstance. By contrast, you are not required to introduce yourself to everyone if you are attending a large meeting.

You should avoid introducing yourself to someone, especially someone influential, only because you wish to introduce yourself to that person. Introduce yourself only if you are confident that that person would be pleased to know you or, of course, the circumstances require you to make a self-introduction. Whatever the circumstances, don't ever interrupt someone to introduce yourself but wait for the opportunity to arise.

What to say

Strictly speaking, best society has only one phrase in acknowledgment of an introduction (whether a third party introduction or a self-introduction) and that is "How do you do?" Best society literally accepts no other and banish, in particular, any form of affectation whatsoever.

Although very much in common use, the expressions "Pleased to meet you" or "Nice to meet you" should be avoided unless you have reason to be sure that the person to whom you are introducing yourself or are being introduced is also genuinely pleased to meet you.

That might be the case, for instance, if you have a friend in common and have long heard of the other person and know that that person also has heard much of you. This may be the case if you have had previous dealings with that person via e-mail or telephone and are meeting them in person for the first time. A good handshake accompanied by an energetic "Very glad to meet you" or "Delighted to meet you" would be the most appropriate form of introduction in these circumstances.

If you are a complete stranger to the person to whom you are introducing yourself, the first acknowledgment should be immediately followed by your full name and a brief statement about who you are and what you do.

Once again, preparation is vital in these instances. If you have not prepared a brief self-introduction statement beforehand you may find it hard to make a pleasant self-introduction on the spot.

You should be selective about the words you use to describe yourself and your work since, especially if you are meeting a potential client or someone who could be a source of referrals, you should make sure that the words you use stick to that person's mind and draw their attention to yourself as much as possible.

Prepare therefore your self-introduction beforehand and make sure that it will provide information you wish to share and also interest others. You may wish to prepare a few different self-introduction statements to be used on different persons. Then practise your self-introduction often until it sounds natural and spontaneous. It may sound trite, but very few people do. Bear in mind that, contrary to what happens in respect of third-party introductions, an awkwardly delivered self-introduction does not receive much appreciation and does not give a good impression at all.

Finally, don't forget to monitor your body language and voice tone when practicing and delivering your self-introduction.

4.   How to Remember Names

Introduction

Being able to remember the name of the persons you meet is evident. Being able to remember peoples' names and pronounce them correctly has many rewards and, if you show the people you meet that you can remember their names, you will appear as someone who cares not only about business but also about the people involved.

Being able to remember the name of someone you meet will be key to establishing a personal relationship with them and laying the ground for receiving a positive response if you follow-up with them.

If you sometimes struggle to remember names, there are a number of things that you can do to improve your memory. To start with, understand the two golden rules of remembering names.

The first golden rule is: you will not be able to remember a name unless you really want to. This means that, is you wish to remember someone's name, you must genuinely want to learn and remember that person's name when that person is introduced to you. In other words, there must be a genuine desire on your part to ascertain and remember that person's name.

It has been observed, in effect, that most of the time forgetting a name is not the result of a poor memory but rather the result of a lack of desire to remember that person's name in the first place. Sometimes a person just cannot be bothered about making the mental effort required to remember another person's name, perhaps just because in their opinion the other person is not "important enough".

From now on, therefore, whenever someone is introduced to you, you may wish to pretend that the person being introduced to you is the most important person in the world. You will be surprised about how effective your memory will be when you are willing to make even a simple effort. And, while you are there, you may wish also to relinquish the mental attitude of classifying the persons you meet in accordance to your perceived importance of them.

The second golden rule is: practise as much as you can. This may sound trite but, once again, it is the truth. Your ability to remember names will improve only if you follow consistently the suggestions explained below and find out the one or ones that work best for you. With the required practice, however, you will soon be able to impress people about you remarkable ability to remember names.

Memory retention techniques

Here are a few suggestions that may help you to remember a name more effectively:

- Ask for the name to be repeated. Repetition will help you even if you did clearly hear that person's name. You will find that people do not get annoyed if you ask for their name to be repeated. They will rather appreciate your effort to understand their name and be most pleased to repeat it for you.

- Ask the person to spell their name. This will typically apply where that person's name is uncommon or is a foreign name. Don't be afraid to ask that person to spell their name for you because, once again, your effort to understand that person's name will be noticed and appreciated. Chances are that person will also know that their name is not easy to understand.

- State the name as soon as possible during the conversation. Say "How do you do, Mr. Senior". It is sometimes said that if you can use a person's name at least three times early in the conversation, you will remember their name. By contrast, repeating a person's name to yourself over and over again is not generally an effective technique to remember a name, especially if you are dealing with a number of people. So don't overdo it unless you know that technique works for you. Muttering the person's name to yourself is also unlikely to work.

- Write down the name. This has proved to be a very successful memorizing technique for the majority of people although obviously it is not always a practicable option. Reading a person's name on a name tag or, even better, on a business card is however equally effective especially if you are a visual learner.

- Associate the name to something common to you. Maybe the name of the person you have just met is the same as a friend of yours, a work colleague or a favourite fictional character. To make this technique really work, you should visually associate the image of the person you have just met to the name of your friend, work colleague etc.

* Associate the name to some unique feature or bizarre mental image. If you have noticed some unique feature in the person whose name you wish to remember, associate the *image* of that unique feature to the *name* of that person. The more you exaggerate the size, shape and action of the associated image the more this technique will be effective. Obviously, since the association will most likely be bizarre and surreal, keep it to yourself and do not share it with the person concerned.

It will be easier to make use of this technique if an association can be easily found in the person concerned. If an association does not come up fairly quickly in your mind, don't struggle too much with this technique since a stretched association will probably not help you remember that name. In those circumstances, you may be better off using one of the other memory retention techniques listed above.

It has been said, however, that this technique is the most powerful existing technique and that the more you practise it the easier the association process will be. With constant practice, you will soon be able to recall any person's name using this technique without thinking much about it.

If you forget a name

From today on you should make it a rule not to talk to any person whose name you have forgotten or do not know. You may have noticed in the past how embarrassing it may be to show someone that you do not remember their name after you have engaged in conversation with them for minutes or even hours. From today on, therefore, don't ignore the fact that you have forgotten the name of the person with whom you are conversing.

If you have forgotten a name, the safest and easiest thing to do is to ask as soon as possible the person concerned to repeat their name for you. You may wish to apologize politely and say that you have forgotten their name. A statement like "I am sorry, I have forgotten your name" will be sufficient and certainly preferable to an abrupt and unflattering "What is your name again?".

Rest assured that, as long as you are polite, the person you are talking to will be most pleased to repeat their name for you.

As a corollary of the rule presented above, from today on you should also avoid introducing a person whose name you have forgotten to someone else in order to find out the first person's name. Whilst it is true that fairly often two persons being introduced to one another each pronounce their name when introduced, this does not always happen and you risk embarrassment if you are not able to say the name of the persons concerned without the need to ask them again. Remember also that, as seen previously in this chapter, the rules of etiquette require you to say first the names of the persons being introduced to one another.

Finally, if you notice that, after you have been introduced to some person, that person starts mispronouncing your name or, even worse, calling you by a wrong name, don't hesitate to correct them in order to avoid mutual embarrassment.

5.   First Name or Title

It is fair to say that nowadays in Britain that there is no longer a requirement to address someone whom you have just met with the title of Mr, Ms, Miss or Mrs in ordinary business dealings.

Despite their reputation for stiff formality, the British are in fact quite informal and the immediate use of first names has become commonplace in a business environment. This contrasts sharply with other countries such as France and Italy where a fairly high degree of formality is still prevalent in both social and business contexts.
However, there are a few exceptions. For example, you should not address a person on a first name basis upon meeting them if that person is a member of the "Establishment", is significantly older then you or covers a significantly more senior position then you. In these

cases, it is better to err on the side of caution and not address them on a first name basis unless explicitly or implicitly invited to do so.

These persons might find premature informality presumptuous or simply inappropriate. They will however not be offended by your formal and respectful manners and in fact might appreciate them quite a lot.

In all these cases, you should address the person you are dealing with using the title appearing on their business card, or given by that person when you were first introduced to them, followed by their surname. In the absence of any professional title, you should use "Mr", "Mrs", "Ms" or "Miss" again followed by their surname.

Certain members of the Establishment – in particular the Government, the military and the academia - are still very much devoted to titles denoting rank or academic achievement and you should accordingly do your best to use the appropriate title when addressing them.

If you are unsure about which title to use, you may wish to consult *Debrett's Correct Form* or any other similar manual beforehand. Unfortunately, there are no universal rules in this matter and whilst certain rules are common knowledge or common sense, others are not.

For example, you may already know that you should address a Knight with the title of "Sir" followed by his first name only. You may not know, by contrast, that you should address a Knight's wife as "Lady" followed by her surname or that you should address a Dame (which is the female equivalent of a Knight) as "Dame" followed by her first name only. Likewise, you should address the daughter of a Duke, Marquis or Earl as "Lady" followed by her first name only.

You might think that the likelihood of dealing with a Knight in the course of your work as a lawyer is small. If you consider however that a knighthood usually recognizes real achievement rather than political patronage, you will soon realize that it might not be that uncommon to meet a Knight in the business world.

As a closing remark on this topic, remember that, unless the *Debrett's Correct Form* requires otherwise, you should never address someone with the titles of "Sir" or "Madam", which are nowadays only used by shop assistants to address their customers. Nor should you address someone with their surname only despite the persistent tradition amongst very close (male) friends, who have usually attended the same public school or ancient university, of doing so.

Lastly, so far as written documents, meetings, conferences etc. are concerned, you should always use full titles even if all the participants would ordinarily be on first-name terms.

6.   Business Cards Etiquette

As a lawyer, you are probably already accustomed to using business cards. This section therefore will simply present a few rules of etiquette concerning the use of business cards in a business context.

A business card should generally be given at the beginning of a meeting, individually to each participant if the circumstances so permit, unless of course you already know them or have done business with them before.

If you are attending a large meeting, you may wish to make sure that you deliver your business card to those persons who might require it most (the lawyers from the other side, other advisers or clients) but make sure that under no circumstances you scatter your cards on a meeting table or throw them to anyone too far away from you. Not only would this be against proper etiquette but it might also be perceived as aggressive behaviour. The same applies, needless to say, whenever you are passing on papers to someone else at a meeting table– never ever throw papers to people.

It is generally acceptable business behaviour to keep the business cards of the people sitting at the meeting in front of you, as long as you keep them tidy and in order among your papers. Doing this will help you remember the names of the other persons at the meeting.

If you are attending a social or networking event and meet someone new there, you should avoid giving them your business card at the beginning of the conversation unless of course you are asked for one or, for example, you are asked to repeat your name in which case showing the spelling of your name on your business card will help the person you have met to understand you name.

It is generally appropriate, by contrast, to give your business card at the end of a conversation prior to leaving, while thanking the other person for the interesting conversation. It is also appropriate, and perhaps necessary, to give your business card if the other person offers to send you something or promises a follow up.

Don't let vanity stop you from giving out your last business card or giving two cards to the same person. Business cards are essentially a marketing tool so you should use them as much use as possible.

Needless to say, you should *always* carry a few business cards with you and carry them in a case to keep them neat. If you do not already have a business card case, get one immediately.

If the other person does not ask for your card, do not volunteer to give them your card. Instead, ask them for their card and reciprocate by giving them your card. Remember that it may not be proper to ask someone far more senior than you for a business card. For example, if you are a junior lawyer you should not ask the senior executive of one of your firm's clients for their card nor offer yours unless asked for.

Whenever you are given a business card, do not just take it and place it in the pocket of your jacket. Instead, look at the card for a few seconds with interest and admiration and make some positive comments if appropriate. You might even see something on the card that could be a topic of discussion. This way you will make the person feel important and demonstrate a sincere interest in them.

You should then place their card in your own business card case rather than simply into your pockets. This will let the other person know that you will conserve their business card neatly in your case and this will be taken as a sign of respect.

Afterwards, when you are back in your office, write comments on the cards you have been given during the event which will help you remember the persons concerned. You might note the date and location of your meeting and the common points of interest you had with those persons. These comments will prove invaluable when following up.

A few more suggestions:

- Insert a business card whenever you are sending parcels, documents, cards or invitations by post. Once again, be generous with your business cards and take every opportunity to distribute them.

- Whenever you give your business card to someone, ask them for a referral. This may sound trite and perhaps even not appropriate for lawyers but don't let this stop you. And if they say they would be pleased to mention you to some business associate or other potential client, give them two or more cards and don't feel ashamed about that.

- The day after you have met someone at a social or networking event, send that person a handwritten note thanking them for their time and how pleasant it was to meet them at the event. Once again, you might find this trite but you will be amazed at the response you will get if you do so.

7.   Social Cards Etiquette

If you really want to impress people with your style and elegance, you should start using social cards. Very few lawyers use them, so this will give you the opportunity to stand out from the crowd and impress clients and colleagues.

Social cards should be of the same size as standard business cards. They should include your full name in the centre (generally without titles) and your telephone number at the lower right corner. You may wish also to add your personal e-mail address but make sure that there is left plenty of blank space on the front of the card for a greeting to be written on it.

Social cards should be used as much as possible with established clients of yours or your firm. If you are an experienced lawyer, you are probably very well aware of the importance of establishing a personal relationship with your clients. Therefore, use your social cards on every occasion and don't forget to include them as gift enclosures or to accompany greeting cards.

In a business context, you may wish to give your social cards (as opposed to your business cards) when you meet colleagues with whom you wish to maintain contact but do not want to appear strictly business. Your colleagues will be positively impressed by your card and will look at it afterwards as if it was a friend's card.

This will help you build a longer-term rapport with them which may prove useful, for instance, if you require their help from a career perspective further down the line.

8.   Chairing a business meeting

In principle, you are expected to chair any meeting or conference call you convene and not let any of the participants to chair the meeting instead, even if they are more senior than you, unless of course the circumstances so require.

If you are chairing a meeting, select a seat where you can see all participants well and make your voice heard and your presence noticed from the beginning.

When the meeting or conference call commences, introduce yourself and then introduce each participant to the others unless they already know each other. Have the meeting's agenda in front of you and present to the meeting which topics will be discussed. Then summarise the main issues concerning the first topic and let the discussion commence.

Facilitate the discussion by taking care of each participant and explicitly seek comments from your client, if they are attending the meeting or conference, so that they feel that they are taken care of and given the opportunity to express their opinion in full. Do not move on to the next topic unless they confirm that they are ready to do so.

Always state formally when the discussion on a topic is closed and then move on by introducing the next topic, until all topics have been dealt with. Then summarise any follow-up or action plan that has been agreed, thank all participants and, unless any of the participants wishes to put forward any additional topic for discussion, declare the meeting closed. Once again, ask your client explicitly if they wish to add anything before closing the meeting.

It is often suggested that a chairman should never let the discussion digress from the agenda items or permit too long or frivolous discussions. This is certainly good advice but remember to be flexible.

9.   Automobile Etiquette

If you are travelling with a more senior lawyer from your office or a client of your firm, you may have wondered whether rules of etiquette exist on automobile travelling and travelling on taxis. A short summary of those rules is provided below.

Who should enter the car first

Etiquette requires that the host should enter the vehicle first so that guests do not have to slide across the seat and so that the host can easily give instructions to the driver. If no formal host/guest relationship exist, the more junior person should enter first and slide over followed by the more senior person or the client.

Where passengers should sit

The preferred passenger seat in an automobile, which should be reserved to the most senior person or the client, is the rear seat on the passenger side. You should therefore invite your senior colleague or client to sit there while you sit next to them on the driver side of the rear seat. But if access to the rear seat is only from one side, you should never have your colleague or client to slide over.

If there are already two passengers sitting on the rear seat, you should sit on the passenger seat on the front next to the driver.

Irrespective of the seating, remember that as the most junior person it will be your responsibility to instruct the driver and do so as discretely as possible without speaking over the other passengers.

Who should leave the car last

The host or more junior person should be the last passenger to leave the vehicle and be responsible for paying the driver.

10. Entertainment and Social Events

Introduction

It is often said that social events can be a great opportunity to further a person's career, ruin their reputation and everything in between.

Social events can give you a unique opportunity to meet and build a relationship with more senior members of your firm, who you perhaps might not have otherwise had the opportunity to meet during normal working hours. At the same time, however, social events can give you a unique opportunity to destroy your good reputation and commit blunders that might have a long-lasting damaging effect on your career.

Due to their apparent relaxed and friendly atmosphere, social events will put you at risk of lowering your defence mechanisms. In other words, you will face a higher risk of failing to maintain the standards of behaviour that are expected of you as a lawyer.

As always, your credibility and professionalism will be on display and your behaviour and words will contribute to determine how you are perceived by the people that surround you. You should always consider the impact that your words and actions will have on the image you want to project. This is particularly important if, as mentioned above, people who may influence you career advancement and future success will be attending the function.

On the other hand, you should not try to appear too controlled or stiff. The function has probably been designed to give you and your colleagues the opportunity to relax and have a good time together outside the office. Under no circumstances should you give the impression of being too much in control, self-conscious or unable to enjoy the event.

Try therefore to strike the right balance between being in control of yourself and being able to relax and enjoy the event. The suggestions contained in the following pages will hopefully help you achieve that balance and help you make the most of any social event whilst still have a good time.

Attendance

You will be generally expected to attend a social function at which you have been invited unless of course there are genuine reasons which prevent you from doing so. You should not decline an invitation only because you do not feel like attending the event concerned, you are simply not interested or do not generally feel at ease at social events with your colleagues.

If you decline too many invitations, you will appear to be antisocial and that will certainly not help you build long-lasting relationships with others.

If you genuinely cannot attend an event, respond to the host with your regrets. You may want to explain the reasons you cannot attend but you do not need to do so. In any case, it is important to respond and thank your host for the kind invitation.

As you are probably aware, if an invitation is marked "RSVP" ("Respondez s'il vous plait"), you will be required to notify the host as to whether you are planning to attend the event or not. By contrast, if an invitation is marked "R.O." ("Regrets Only"), you will be required to notify the host only if you are unable to attend. In the latter case, if you do not contact the host, you will be expected to attend.

Guests

If you are given the opportunity to attend a function with a guest or other halve, carefully consider the person you are planning to take to the function with you. If your intended date tends to party a little too hearty, you may wish to have a serious talk with them beforehand. And, if you are not confident that they can behave appropriately, it may be safer to bring someone else or attend on your own. The same applies if you have met your partner only recently and are still getting to know them well.

Preparation

Needless to say, preparation will be key to success. Before attending the event, you should gain an appropriate understanding of the type of event concerned and, if the event represents something new to you, gather as much information as possible as to what it is about and how it is likely to develop. Often, a quick search on the internet will provide you with all the information you need.

Depending on the formality of the event, you may also wish to gather information about the etiquette surrounding it and the people you are likely to meet there.

On the basis of the information you have gathered, you will then be able to decide confidently what to wear, whom to take, what to eat, whether to drink, whom to talk to, what to talk about, and when to arrive and leave.

So far as dressing is concerned, social events and other forms of business entertainment are typically an extension of work which means that you should in principle always wear a businesslike party attire. Make sure you dress up from your everyday office uniform but don't go any further than that, unless of course the circumstances so require (e.g. a sporting or casual event). Remember that the wrong outfit can dispel, at a single glance, all your work credibility.

Arrival

Social functions are not the time to be fashionably late. You should arrive at a party or other casual gathering shortly after the event is scheduled to begin but arrive as punctual as possible if the function is a dinner party or other event when you are expected to arrive at the stated time.

At the event

Once at the event, let your guiding principle be Saint Ambrose's dictum, "when in Rome, do as the Romans do". Observe the atmosphere of the event and the behaviour of those attending and ensure that you match that atmosphere and behaviour as much as possible. If you are a guest, follow the lead of your hosts and you will not get it wrong.

Have a fun time but avoid letting your defences down. Cause neither embarrassment nor annoyance and practise your best manners and proper etiquette at every opportunity. Don't get too personal in conversation. Don't complain about business colleagues or gossip. Don't use profanity or tell inappropriate jokes. Don't say anything suggestive and don't flirt.

Whilst keeping your behaviour and words under control, don't forget to enjoy yourself and bring happiness and harmony to the party. And if you would rather be at home washing the dishes, ignore that feeling and still keep bringing happiness and harmony to the party.

Use your time to get to know your colleagues better but avoid discussing overly personal matters or asking impertinently personal questions. At the same time, try to avoid having long or detailed business discussions with your colleagues, unless of course these are initiated by more senior members of your firm. Make a point of meeting any prominent member of your firm attending the event and spend at least five-ten minutes talking to them.

Don't forget that relationships are the bedrock of any career success. So make the most of your time and socialize as much as possible with everyone.

Eating and Drinking

You should monitor how, what, and how much you eat at a social function. If you tend to eat too much, you may wish to have something to eat beforehand or, if your overeating is a reaction to a state of nervousness, keep your nervousness under control.

At a cocktail-type party, you may need to eat standing up. Circulate throughout the party and return to the food periodically rather than stationing in front of the food tables throughout the evening. Try to keep one hand free to shake hands and do not overly fill dishes with food.

So far as drinking is concerned, it might be too strict to expect you to skip any alcoholic drink altogether. That would certainly appear excessive and might give your colleagues the impression that you are too stiff and do not wish to relax and enjoy the event with them.

This said, you should certainly keep your alcohol consumption under control and perhaps alternate alcoholic drinks with non-alcoholic ones. In between alcoholic drinks, you might try some sparkling water with a slice of lemon or lime, a juice, a virgin drink or a ginger beer.

You may wish to accompany your alcoholic drinks with some food, in particular foods that are high in carbohydrates or protein, which will help you absorb the alcohol. By contrast, try to avoid salty or greasy foods because these may make you want to drink more.

Lastly, try to keep your glass in your left hand so that your handshake is not wet and cold (use your right hand, of course, if you are left-handed).

Leaving

You should leave the event as soon as the festivities begin to ebb. Do not close down the party. And be sure to talk to the host before leaving to thank them for the event.

After the Event

Send a thank you note to the host after the event, ideally the following day. A simple handwritten note or humorously worded e-mail message will do. You should acknowledge the host and the good time you shared at their event and thank them once again.

Remedying gaffes

If you have committed a blunder or gaffe at the event, you should take a view as to the seriousness of the matter and how you can remedy it. You should apologise in person or write a note of apology if your behaviour at the event has been inappropriate to a material extent or has caused significant embarrassment. By contrast, if your behaviour was less serious, you may be better off by not doing anything so as not to draw your attention to your errant behaviour.

11. Dining Etiquette

Table manners play an important part in making a favourable impression upon colleagues and clients. They are visible signals of the state of your manners generally. Regardless of whether you are having lunch with a prospective client or dinner with a colleague, your table manners will speak volumes about your professionalism.

As a well-educated lawyer, you are probably aware of the rules of etiquette governing dining situations. You may however find the following paragraphs as a useful refresher on the topic.

Posture

The importance of keeping a straight yet relaxed and friendly posture has been highlighted previously in this book. The suggestions given there apply, *mutatis mutandis*, to dining situations.

At the dining table, sit straight and keep your elbows off the table. Throughout the dinner, remember the golden rule "elbows never, forearms sometimes, wrists always". You are unlikely to maintain an inappropriate posture at the dining table as long as you do not slouch when seated at any time during the dinner.

As a relaxation to the golden rule, you may keep your hands on your lap when you are not eating, although resting your hands on the table with wrists on the edge of the table would still be preferable. Elbows on the table may acceptable between courses, after dishes have been cleared by the waiter, but again try always to keep your elbows off the table if you can. As always, follow the lead of the host in this respect.

If you are a man, keep your jacket on unbuttoned at the table and remove it only in an informal situation and always provided that the host has suggested that you do so.

Mobile Phones

Turn off you mobile phone, Blackberry or PDA. Contrary to popular belief, you can survive an hour without them. If you are on call and need to keep it switched on, alert your host and guests as soon as you sit down.

If the phone rings, excuse yourself from the table and keep your conversation private and brief. Do not remain at the table or cover your mouth while talking. If you have a Blackberry or PDA with you and wish to check your messages from time to time, leave the table and move to a private place.

The general principle is that whenever you are at the dining table with someone, you should devote your undivided attention to them.

Bread & Butter

Especially if you are not British, you may be unfamiliar with the etiquette surrounding the use of bread & butter at the dining table.

To start with, remember the rule "solids on your left, liquids on your right": your bread plate and cutlery will be on your left-hand side whilst your glasses will be on your right-hand side. This should help you remember the place settings and avoid embarrassing situations.

If you wish to have some bread & butter, you should first take a serving of butter from the butter dish and put the butter on your bread plate. Then break from the bread a bite-size piece, spread the butter onto it and eat it. Then repeat the same process if you wish to eat more bread.

Similar rules apply whenever you are eating bread or rolls with a spread. Always put the spread on a small bite size piece and repeat the process until you have finished. Never spread a whole roll or bread as if you were preparing a sandwich.

Napkin Use

You should put your napkin on your lap as soon as you sit down at the dinner table although, if you are a guest, you may also follow the lead of your host and only unfold your napkin when the host unfolds theirs.

Place your napkin on your lap, completely unfolded if it is a small luncheon napkin or in half, lengthwise, if it is a large dinner napkin. Keep the napkin there throughout the entire meal and gently use the napkin to clean your mouth when needed.

Do not tuck in your napkin, unless of course you are at a kids' party, and don't fidget with it during the meal. If you need to leave the table during the meal, place your napkin on your chair as a signal to your waiter that you will be returning.

It will be the responsibility of the host to signal the end of the meal by placing their napkin on the table. Once again, follow the lead of the host and place your napkin neatly on the table to the right of your dinner plate. Do not refold your napkin but make sure it is tidied left on the table.

Cutlery

Choosing the correct piece of cutlery from the variety in front of you is not as difficult as it may first seem, even if you are at the most formal dinner with dozen of pieces around you. Just remember to "work your way from outside in" using one utensil for each course.

Your salad fork will typically be the outermost piece on the left whilst your soupspoon will be on your outermost right, followed by your salad knife and dinner knife. Your dessert utensils, a spoon and/or a fork, will be above your plate or brought with the dessert.

So far as using the cutlery is concerned, there are two styles of using knife and fork to cut and eat your food. They are the American style and the European or Continental style.

In the American style, you would be cutting a few bite-size pieces of food first by holding your knife in your right hand and your fork in your left hand, then lay your knife across the top edge of your plate with the sharp edge of the blade facing in, change your fork from your left to your right hand and start eating your food.

In the European or Continental style, by contrast, you would keep your fork in your left hand and the knife in your right hand throughout the meal and eat the cut pieces of food by picking them up with your fork soon after you have cut them.

Either style is considered appropriate so feel free to use the style that you find most suitable to you.

If you are engaged in conversation during the meal and not eating, you should place the utensils on the dish in the shape of an inverted

V, the so called "resting position" which signal the waiter that you have not finished eating.

If during the meal a piece of your utensils falls onto the floor, pick it up if you can reach it and politely ask the waiter to bring you a clean one. If you cannot reach your utensil, simply let the waiter know what happened and ask them to bring you a clean one.

Once you have used a piece of cutlery, never place it back on the table. Do not leave a used spoon in a cup, either, but place it on the saucer. You can leave a soupspoon in a soup plate.

At the end of the meal, place the utensils diagonally across your plate, the so called "closed position" which signals the waiter that you have finished eating, even if there is still some food on your plate. Make sure they are placed in such a way that they do not slide off the plate as it is being removed.

Ordering

You should order your food with utmost care when dining out on business and order only food that is easy to eat with a knife and fork. Resist the temptation of ordering any finger food, soup and shelled seafood. These may taste great but may be messy to eat and expose you to the risk of having your tie and shirt decorated by bits of sauce.

If, after looking at the menu, there are dishes you are uncertain about, you may ask the waiter any questions you may have or ask them to give you general suggestions as to what to order. Be aware about the "dish of the day" though. There are still contrasting views as to whether that is the best dish on the menu or the worse – insiders swear that the dish of the day was created to make good use of all the food and ingredients that have been left over the past few days at the restaurant.

If you are the host, invite your guests to give their orders first. The host is generally the last to order although sometimes the waiter will decide how the ordering will proceed and perhaps take women's orders first.

If you are a guest, avoid ordering one of the most expensive items on the menu or more than two courses unless your host encourages you to do so.

So far as drinks are concerned, try to avoid ordering alcoholic drinks altogether, especially if you are at a business lunch. If ordering wine is appropriate, ask the waiter for suggestions before ordering and sample the wine for flavour when the bottle is served. In rare cases, you may refuse the wine because it is spoiled. However, you may not refuse it if you do not like its taste.

When to talk about business

There are contrasting opinions as to when is the right moment to start talking about business if you are at a business lunch. Certain authors suggest that business conversation should not commence before the conclusion of the mains, which essentially means that business topics should be addressed only over dessert and coffee. Other authors maintain however that it is perfectly fine to entertain business conversation at any time during the meal since a business lunch is essentially a business meeting at lunchtime.

As always, use your judgment and decide, on a case-by-case basis, when is the most appropriate time to commence a business conversation. Whatever you decide to do, do it confidently and you won't get it wrong.

Keep in mind that it will generally be inappropriate to place business papers on the table before business discussion has commenced. Even after business discussion has started, keep the table as clutter free as possible and only place on the table the materials that are strictly necessary.

Toasts

Toasts are always appropriate at a business lunch or dinner when celebrating completion of a project or the victory of a trial case.

If you are the host, you may wish to prepare a brief speech or statement for the occasion. Remember though that the purpose of a toast is to compliment and acknowledge the event and your guests and not to bore them with your own philosophy of business or the secrets of your success. In addition, you should never give a toast in respect of events which are long passed, future achievements or individuals who are not present at the occasion. A simple statement like "We are glad to be able to celebrate the successful completion of our project together" will often do.

After the speech has closed, the toaster is the first to sip, followed by the guests. If however the toast is given in honour of a person present, that person should not sip but only nod in acknowledgment. In return, they may reciprocate with their own toast.

So far as touching glasses is concerned, follow the lead of the toaster and, in case of doubt, refrain from touching glasses unless others do so. Touching glasses will be more acceptable in less formal environments.

Gaffes to avoid

In case you are in doubt, the following are not acceptable behaviours at a business dinner:
- Coughing without covering your mouth.
- Burping even if you say "excuse me"
- Yawning
- Speaking with your mouth full
- Getting out a mirror at the table
- Stretching across the table
- Eat and drink at exceedingly fast or slow pace
- Waving your cutlery about
- Licking your knife or using your knife to take food to your mouth
- Slurp soup from a spoon
- Blow on hot food to let it cool
- Pushing your plate away from you when you have finished eating
- Ask for a doggy bag or take the wine away with you

71

Food Incidents

If food gets caught between your teeth and you can't remove it discreetly with your tongue, excuse yourself and go to the lavatories.

If you eat a piece of bad food, do not spit it into your napkin. Instead, remove the food from your mouth using the same utensil it went in with, place the piece of food on the edge of your plate and, if possible, cover it with some other food from your plate.

If food spills off your plate, pick it up with your fork and place it on the edge of your plate.

Leaving the table

You should not leave the table during the meal except in an emergency. If you must go to the lavatory or if you suddenly become sick, simply excuse yourself and go. Later you can apologize to the host by saying that you didn't feel well.

Payment

If you are the host, tip generously and sincerely compliment the staff for their excellent service. This augurs well for future visits.

12. Dealing with the Disabled

You may have had dealings with disabled people at work and felt awkward about not knowing how best to acknowledge and treat them. If that is the case, the following suggestions, which are provided by a number of organisations (including MD Support, Apparelyzed and others), will be able to help you.

When dealing with the disabled, remember always to smile, be gracious, show respect and give them the dignity they deserve. Always demonstrate patience and, for example, if you are hosting a meeting at which disabled individuals will attend, make sure all necessary arrangements are in place to cater for their needs and allow extra time for your meeting so that they will not feel rushed. Your extra care and effort will be greatly appreciated.

Shaking hands

If you are meeting for the first time someone who has lost their right hand, you may wish to greet them by touching them lightly on the wrist, forearm or shoulder. This warm gesture, accompanied by your smile, will be the best way to greet them.

Offer to shake the disabled person's hand or touch them even if they appear to have limited use of their arms or hands. This action of personal contact will break any psychological barrier of non-acceptance and create a warmer environment of communication.

Wheelchair bound

If you are engaging in conversation with a person in a wheelchair, try not to make them look up at you for the duration of the conversation. Instead, sit in a chair or kneel if possible so that you will be closer to the same eye level.

Ignore the wheelchair during the conversation as much as you can and, if the disabled person has thin legs due to wasted muscle mass or a pot belly due to paralysis of the abdominal muscles, try not to keep looking at their legs or belly. Remember that you are talking to the person and not their disability.

Hearing impaired

If you wish to talk to a hearing-impaired individual, you may wish to get their attention so that they are looking at you. Some hearing-impaired individuals are able to read lips and understand much of what is being said as long as they can see the speaker's face.

Visually impaired

If you are meeting a visually impaired individual, face them directly and speak clearly. Introduce yourself so they will know who is talking to them and touch them gently on the arm as a sign of greeting.

Speak to them as you would speak to a sighted person, at a normal level and enunciate your words well. Don't get distracted and don't hesitate if they eyes weave during the conversation and, more importantly, make sure that you always face them directly. Visually impaired individuals generally have a very acute hearing and will notice it immediately if, whilst talking to them, you do something else or are otherwise distracted.

Remember also to announce your presence whenever you are nearby and let them know if you are leaving the room. If other people join you, introduce them to the visually impaired person without delay as you would with any other visitor.

Whilst talking to a blind person, do not apologise if you use an expression such as "See you later". These expressions are part of everyday language and the apology will probably be more offensive or embarrassing that the expression.

Speech impaired

You will need to be patient and extra attentive with speech-impaired individuals and be careful not to finish their sentences or thoughts for them. As with any other person, it will be impolite to finish the sentences or otherwise interrupt any speech-impaired individual. Instead, give them all the time they need to express themselves in full.

If you wish to facilitate the conversation, you may help by asking questions that only require a yes or no answer or an otherwise brief answer but, again, do not ever finish their sentences of or otherwise interrupt them.

13.   Gift Giving

Proper gift giving will help you build strong and durable relationships with your colleagues and clients. Giving a gift to a colleague or friend is a demonstration that you care about them and consider them highly. As such, it will generate goodwill with the recipient, as long as you have selected and presented an appropriate business gift.

It is fair to say that every occasion may be a suitable occasion to present a gift. For example, you may bring a gift to your colleagues on returning from a trip abroad or to celebrate your colleague's promotion.

Business gifts are not generally exchanged at Christmas where it may be more appropriate to simply send a card. If you are sending a Christmas card, make sure that it is not received too far in advance of Christmas day and contains a personal greeting. An impersonal message on a Christmas card will leave the recipient unimpressed.

When selecting a gift, remember that gifts should never be too cheap, ostentatiously expensive or personal. They should always be consumable, attractive and easily transportable.

A bottle of good champagne, for example, has become more and more acceptable as a gift and has actually become a very common gift to give to junior colleagues to thank them for their services.

Other alcoholic beverages, by contrast, should be avoided. Spirits, for example, are a matter of personal taste. If a bottle of your favourite whisky is not also your recipient's favourite, it will languish in their cabinet for years to come.

Other suitable gifts include a case of fine chocolates, local edible products, coffees and teas or regional items.

Make sure that your gifts are well presented and give them privately. If you are sending your gift to the recipient, include a handwritten note to accompany your gift and enclose your social card.

If you receive a gift, don't forget to reciprocate. If you feel that the circumstances so permit, the best way to reciprocate for a gift received is to invite the giver to dinner or other entertainment event to enjoy together.

CHAPTER 5 – HOW TO BECOME A PARTNER

This chapter contains a number of suggestions that will help you become a partner in your firm. You will find this chapter particularly useful if you are a junior lawyer or a trainee working in a large City firm.

The suggestions provided in this chapter will hopefully help you achieve your partnership goals.

1.   Partnership pursuit begins day one

If you wish to become a partner in a large firm, you have to start working on achieving your goal from the day you walk into your firm for the very first time. As you probably know, the path to partnership is a long one so, if you are serious about becoming a partner, you will have to work on it from the very beginning.

The partnership track at most major law firms is nowadays seven to ten years long. You should use every single day of this period to prepare yourself for that position because, if you procrastinate and fail to seriously consider how to prepare yourself for partnership from the very beginning, you may find that it is has become too late, surprisingly quickly. Preparation for partnership will mean, most of the time, making an organised and concerted effort to acquire every single skill which is required of a partner.

As already explained, partnership is not only about technical capabilities. Being a partner requires the possession of a much wider range of skills which can only be acquired through a long period of learning and practice. Being excellent in your practice area will not guarantee you professional success – it is very possible to be professional, proficient and unemployed.

Take the time, therefore, to identify the skills that may really bring you success within your firm and make a realistic plan for acquiring those skills. Then start implementing your plan straight away.

You may already know, for example, that partners have a number of non-billable administrative responsibilities and may be in charge of management areas such as money laundering, compliance, information technology and office systems, recruitment or training, etc.

If you wish to improve your partnership prospects, you should start getting interested in all these management areas early on in your career so as to be able to show a strong familiarity with management functions by the time you get in the "partnership zone". Your management capabilities will give you an edge over all the other associates who have not acquired similar competencies.

Similar considerations apply to all other non-legal skills such as communication, project management and delegation, negotiation and business development. Make a realistic plan for acquiring these skills early on in you career and you will gain a distinct advantage.

Remember, no matter where you are in your career, don't make the mistake of thinking that it is too early to think about partnership. Work on your partnership goal from the day you start at your firm and you will be half way there.

2.   Think like an owner

It has been suggested that the educational system today is heavily tailored towards creating perfect employees as opposed to business owners.

A perfect employee is someone who is hard-working and meticulous, who arrives at the office on time every morning and feels content and fulfilled on leaving the office in the evening if they have carried out with utmost diligence and care the duties that have been assigned to them by their employer. Someone who is well behaved, always respects their colleagues, who obeys all instructions by superiors and who does not take an initiative on their own. Someone who thinks in terms of payslips, annual reviews, and expects pay rises and benefits.

If you wish to become a partner in your firm, you have to stop thinking like a perfect employee and start thinking like an owner.

An owner is someone who knows that doing their job with utmost diligence and care is not sufficient. Someone who knows that obeying instructions is not all that is required of them. And, more importantly, someone who is accustomed to put in extra effort despite knowing that 90% of the time there will be no return for their extra work.

You should understand that a law firm is a business venture and, like all ventures, does not have any guaranteed future. A firm can be a perfectly viable and profitable business one day, and become unprofitable and go out of business the day after.

If you wish to become a partner, you should start taking responsibility for the present and future success of your firm and stop thinking that, if you were to find yourself working for an unprofitable firm, you would simply leave and find another job.

You should become aware of the business reality of practising law and be willing to take full responsibility for the present and future success of your firm. You should understand that there is no guaranteed future for any firm.

In addition, you should educate yourself in business, including accounting and management. Whether you find these topics interesting or not, you should learn how to read financial statements and management accounts, monitor key performance indicators and identify financial trends.

If you are a not corporate lawyer, and do not therefore already have a good working knowledge of accounting and management, consider taking a class on those topics or studying against a relevant qualification.

Whatever your area of expertise, make sure that you are highly numerate and proficient in business accounting. If you wish to become a partner, you really need to understand how a business works.

You should also understand that one of the most important responsibilities of a partner is to make rain, whether you find this prospect attractive or not. This means overcoming any shyness or psychological resistance you might have developed as a consequence of your education.

If you are an assistant working in a large City firm, you will probably have attended schools and universities that trained you on how to do work that is assigned to you brilliantly but not how to find that work by yourself.

Be aware that this will be a major limitation further down your career path unless you learn the relevant skill. The sections in this book on business development will hopefully help you in this respect but, depending on your situation, you may wish to integrate this book with other specific books or courses.

In summary, open your eyes to the business reality of practising law and start feeling responsible for the success of your firm. The more senior people in your organisation will notice your renewed attitude and will start looking at you more as a business associate than a fungible employee.

If you are able to show business awareness and concern for the future of your firm, you will be perceived by the more senior people at your firm as someone to whom they know they can entrust the future of the firm. This will be more empowering for you and dramatically increase your partnership prospects.

3. Learn to Play Office Politics

Politics are part of human dynamics and play a major role in every social grouping. They are a biological reality of human nature and are as instinctive as the basic needs of eating and sleeping. By nature, people are favourably biased towards people they know, like and trust, even when they are trying to be impartial.

As a gathering of several individuals, a firm is not immune from office politics. Office politics are a reality of every firm at all hierarchical levels and, as you may expect, the larger the firm the more significant the role office politics will play in the day-to-day life of the firm.

If you want to further your career within any firm, you will need to learn how to play office politics wisely. You cannot afford to ignore this reality, whether you like it or not. Staying away from office politics is generally a big mistake.

You probably know of at least a few instances where not particularly bright associates have risen to the partnership ranks while more competent ones have not. If that happened, it is probably because those associates knew how to play office politics and worked their way up through relationship building more than hard work.

You will generally not be able to succeed purely on your merits. The right personality and the ability to build strong relationships with your colleagues and superiors will be as important as (and sometimes more important than) your technical skills and hard work. And if you manage to combine the two sets of skills you will probably have guaranteed a promotion to partnership very soon.

Learning to play office politics wisely, though, has nothing to do with playing dirty tricks at the expense of others, like being derogatory about a colleague, taking credit for other people's work, criticizing other lawyers or superiors, spreading negative gossip and so on. Fortunately, these kinds of office politics are short lived and backfire in any type of professional organization.

If you find that any of your colleagues is actively engaged in dirty office politics, do not respond. Rest assured that, sooner or later, your colleague's behaviour will backfire and abruptly end their career with the firm. Any career advantage gained through deception is generally short-lived in any professional organization.

The suggestions contained in the following pages will help you succeed in office politics and build, over time, strong relationships with your colleagues and superiors.

Identify the balance of power

Observe how the power is distributed among the present partners of your firm and how the different partners interact with each other. Try to identify the relationships which exist between partners or group of partners. The partners who are responsible for originating and/or supervising the most high profile and profitable matters will likely be the most powerful in your firm.

Understand the generational differences existing among partners and the weight attached to seniority. More senior partners do not necessarily have the most power.

Ask senior colleagues to tell you about the history of your firm and how things evolved into the present situation. Ask them to tell you when and how the more influential partners acquired their power and why other partners left the firm.

Identify who the most successful emerging partners are and try to visualize how the balance of power will have shifted in 5 and 10 years' time.

Once you have gathered the above information, you can start to position yourself wisely. To start with, make sure that you never interfere with the relationships between partners or unintentionally create embarrassment or conflict.

Then choose your mentors wisely. You should ideally be working for the most powerful partners because these will be the partners whose opinions will carry the most weight when it comes to partnership decisions. Do not invest your time and energy backing emerging partners who you do not believe will become tomorrow's heavyweights.

If you are not currently working for the most influential partners, you may want to devise a plan to achieve this. Gradually get to know those partners and let them know that you would like to work for them if the right opportunity arises. Volunteer to assist them on some of their big matters.

The same considerations apply so far as clients are concerned. Try so far as possible to work for the clients who are the most important to the success of your firm or generate the most significant fees. Avoid spending your time working for minor clients who do not have significant growth potential.

Once again, if you find that you are not currently working for the most important clients, make sure that you devise a plan to achieve this. Work on acquiring expertise in an area that is useful in carrying out the type of work that is most required by those clients and make yourself available to help when required.

Don't Gossip

You should never get involved in office gossip. Office gossip is one of the biggest plagues of today's office environment. At best, it wastes time and resources. At worse, it can cause significant disruption and destroy the harmony of an entire organization.

The spreaders of rumour and gossip are eventually caught and often punished. They can even get dismissed. You should therefore stay away from any form of office gossip at all costs and not get involved into any sort of rumour even if it directly concerns you.

Be the last to know. If a rumour reaches you, don't give it any credit or act upon it – chances are you will make a bad decision as a result. Don't try to investigate rumours or seek further information. Don't query a rumour with the person concerned or the spreader of the rumour. Don't let people tell you something if they say that it is a rumour and you should keep it secret.

Don't gossip yourself and especially don't say anything bad about anyone. You should try to avoid making any comment whatsoever about other people in your firm and management decisions. Don't complain and don't assume that anything you say will stay secret.

You are only allowed to comment about other people if you are genuinely praising them for the excellent work they have done. Otherwise, keep all your thoughts to yourself. Gossiping is the perfect way to make enemies within your firm and spoil working relationships.

If someone asks you if you know anything about a rumour concerning your firm or anyone working for your firm, simply say "I don't know". Give the same answer if someone asks for your opinion on something concerning your firm or anyone working for it. Practise saying "I don't know" in response to all gossip or people related questions and you will never regret it.

Don't make enemies

You should never make enemies within your firm nor burn bridges with anyone. Associates with even one important enemy often do not become partners since their promotion might be a source of internal conflicts.

If you wish to avoid making enemies, even if unintentionally, remember never to make others look bad. Don't ever draw other people's attention to a colleague's failings and don't ever criticize or belittle a colleague's work. Instead, try to help your colleague to remedy their failings or improve any piece of work requiring improvement. Discrediting or criticizing your colleagues will not make you look any better.

Take care of your boss

You should always give full support to your boss and make them look good in every situation. Keep an eye on their work and raise any issues you might notice. Query any points which you believe could be improved so that the final product is of the utmost quality.

Don't ever let your boss make a mistake and be there to remedy their failings or weaknesses when required. Update your boss on the latest developments on a matter if they did not have the time to do that by themselves prior to entering a meeting. And if your boss has weak public speaking skills, assist them throughout their presentation.

The more you make your boss look good the more they will want you to stay around.

Be a credit maker

Always give everyone full credit for the work they do and praise the person concerned in front of colleagues and superiors. Don't be afraid of sharing the credit for a project with all your team members.

If you give proper credit to your team members, and you become known as a credit maker, you will gain immense popularity within your firm and will secure the full support of your team members in future. Your colleagues and subordinates will give you all their support if they know that they will be recognized, appreciated and praised for the work they do.

Don't make the mistake of thinking that if you make your team members look too good, your efforts will be diminished. In fact, the opposite is true. Credit takers are often insecure, dishonest and get ultimately found out.

Small things count

Don't underestimate the importance of small things like getting your time-sheets on time every week or signing-out and promptly returning any book you take from the library or informing your firm's reception and your secretary if you will be out of office for any length of time.

Failure to comply with these apparently minor duties generally gives a very bad impression to your superiors and may waste the time of your firm's staff. You will give the impression of being sloppy and not caring about other people and the firm's policies, and this is not the kind of impression you want to give to your colleagues.

4. Work on building relationships

If you want to become a partner of your firm, you have to start investing your time and energy into building strong trusting relationships with everyone working at the firm, be they your superiors, colleagues, subordinates or support staff. Without strong support from the people with whom you work, you will not be able to advance your career.

The relationships you build with your superiors will ensure that you are offered the right opportunities to advance your career. The relationships you build with all your colleagues, subordinates and support staff will ensure that you are able to deliver on those opportunities.

If you fail to build strong and durable relationships with all the people working at your firm, sooner or later you will find that you are not given the support you need to carry out your job efficiently and deliver quality work to your clients. It is the support you are given by the people at your firm that makes things happen, whether you realise it or not. Without that support, you will not be able to achieve long-term success.

Don't be afraid therefore to spend time and energy into building the relationships that you need so much. You should spend at least 15 minutes every day communicating with your co-workers, showing genuine interest in their activities and thanking them for all the support they give you.

You may wish to take your co-workers out for lunch from time to time to show your appreciation. Or invite them for a drink after work or to play a round of golf together, depending on your mutual interests. Every idea will be fine as long as you can show genuine appreciation.

So far as time is concerned, you should realise that investing your time into building relationships will never be a waste. Don't think, therefore, that you are "too busy" to spend time with your co-workers, unless of course you are *really* under pressure and exceptional circumstances apply.

Most internal meetings, for example, are an incredible waste of time if you look solely at their content and what they achieve. They give you, however, the opportunity to meet and greet your co-workers and spend time together, and this will be most valuable from a relationship building point of view. You should never decline an invitation to attend a meeting or show disinterest or annoyance.

Likewise, you should never decline if someone, irrespective of their position, invites you for lunch or to have a quick snack or coffee together. Unless you are *really* under pressure, accepting the invitation will prove in the long term more important than early completion of the assignment at hand. If you refuse the invitation, you will probably be able to complete that assignment earlier but may fail to complete a future assignment altogether.

Remember that when you need a relationship, it is too late to build it. No one will help you if you are in need unless they really care about you and no one will really care about you unless you have shown that you really care about them. Don't be surprised therefore if the people you have not considered much in the past will let you down when you most need them. You will not get out of a relationship more than you have invested into it.

This applies to everyone within your firm, whether they are your superiors, subordinates or colleagues. It will be easier to have the support of your co-workers if you have always treated them pleasantly and respectfully and have always taken the time to greet them with enthusiasm and appreciate them for their work. And the easier you make it for your co-workers to do their job, the easier they will make it for you to do yours.

When the time comes to make your partnership consideration, all the time, energy and money you invested into relationship building will eventually pay off. Once again, the relationships you build with your superiors will ensure that you are offered the right opportunities to advance your career while the relationships you build with all your colleagues, subordinates and support staff will ensure that you are able to deliver on those opportunities.

5.   Toot Your Own Horn

If you wish to become a partner, you have to learn the art of self-promotion, that is the art of gaining visibility within your firm, among your colleagues and superiors. Self-promotion is an essential component of any career-development strategy and a crucial soft skill in today's work environment, especially if you work in a large firm.

Working hard and performing at a high level, billing huge number of hours and working late at night will not get you anywhere if you fail to show your achievements and talents.

Your successes will not get noticed unless you publicize them and spending all your time hidden in the library working hard will certainly not gain you much publicity. Don't believe that if you do a good job, you will automatically be recognised for that and get all the credit you deserve. That won't happen unless you actively work at it.

Your hard work will be virtually worthless if no one notices it, whether a client or a partner of your firm. As explained in the communication sections of this book, success is a matter of perception so if you wish to become successful you have to work on being perceived as such by other people. Your aim is to be perceived by your clients and the partners of your firm as someone who is thriving and on the way up.

In particular, you should appreciate that, especially if you work in a large firm, you need to market yourself within your firm as well as to your firm's clients or potential clients. Advancing your career within a large firm will depend upon the image you project to the existing partners of the firm. If you do not keep them informed about your talents and successes, you will not get noticed and promoted.

Most of the time, your colleagues and superiors will not see you in action, especially if you do not work under their direct supervision. It will be your responsibility to appraise them about your progress and achievements. The more you do that, the more they will perceive you as successful and talented.

Take every opportunity to appraise your colleagues and superiors about what you are up to and draw their attention to your achievements whenever you can. Don't make the mistake of thinking that your behaviour will be improper and you will be perceived as someone full of themselves or showing-off. Remember that promoting yourself is a necessity if you wish to become a partner.

6.   Toot Your Own Horn: Practical Suggestions

The following are practical suggestions that will help you to promote yourself effectively with your colleagues and superiors.

Speak-up about yourself effectively

When you talk to your colleagues and superiors, mention what you're currently doing or have recently done. Tell them what your short-term and long-term goals are and how you're working towards achieving them. State your activities and your most recent accomplishments.

Doing this will give your colleagues and superiors the impression that you are an active and very determined person. You will come across as someone dynamic and always on the go. Stating your goals will impress your colleagues and superiors and achieving them will confirm to them that you are a successful person.

Speak about your accomplishments in definite terms. Don't minimize your successes for the sake of modesty. Don't diminish their importance. Don't qualify your statements with "but", "it was nothing" or "it wasn't as difficult as it might seem". Simply state what you have achieved or what you are set to achieve and let your deeds speak for themselves.

Articles, updates and presentations

Prepare brief articles about topics you have recently dealt with as part of your work or recent updates in the law and send copies of those articles to all the partners and senior colleagues who might be interested in the relevant topic.

Make sure that your articles are brief and succinct otherwise they might not be read. If it is not possible to summarize the relevant topic in half a page or so, make sure that your articles open with a suitable one-paragraph abstract.

If your firm publishes an in-house newsletter, add your articles to that newsletter and ensure that your name appears in the newsletter as often as possible. That will show that you are enthusiastic about your work and willing to share your knowledge and contribute to your firm's success.

Likewise, send to all appropriate partners and senior colleagues copies of any article published by a newspaper or magazine that they might find interesting and directly relevant to their work. Your colleagues will appreciate that you are thinking of them and keeping them informed. Of course, ensure that the articles you send are really relevant and brief.

Offer to organize presentations and internal talks about topics you have recently researched as part of your work or to discuss the issues you have encountered while dealing with a particularly complex transaction or matter. Involve all the members of your team who are willing to contribute in organizing the presentation.

Remember to make your presentation short. The shorter your presentation, the easier it will be for you to prepare and deliver it. Start preparing your presentation as soon as the relevant transaction or matter completes, so that its details and the relevant issues are still fresh in your mind.

Divulge your Successes

Divulge internally every success you achieve at work, such as favourable rulings, completion of successful projects, new client wins and so on. Once again, speak-up about these effectively with your colleagues and superiors and, if you can, publicize them in you firm's in-house newsletter or through a short note from yourself.

Needless to say, the higher the profile of the case, the higher the attention it will draw. Sometimes, the sheer value of a case will ensure high visibility. You should therefore seek to work on high-profile assignments as much as you can.

As far as seeking such assignments is concerned, if you do not have the right skills and relevant experience you are not necessarily precluded from getting them. Explain to the assigning partner that you are looking for a chance to develop your skills and that, once you have had such an opportunity, you will be able to make an even larger contribution to your firm's practice.

Unrelated Matters

Promoting yourself is not only about divulging your professional achievements and work-related successes. It is also about divulging achievements and goals that relate to your personal life. As long as these are meaningful to you, they will be meaningful for the colleagues and superiors who care about you.

Don't be afraid, therefore, to speak-up about what you're currently doing or have recently done and, generally, what is happening in your life even if it is something completely unrelated to work.

Your superiors will generally be interested to hear that you have an active life outside work, that you have a family and what your interests are. The more they know you, the more they will trust and respect you. The more they care about you, the more they will be eager to know about you.

Examples of this are an engagement or marriage, children, buying a flat, participation in charity events or community activities, studying towards a diploma or a new qualification, people whom you have met, travels and so on.

Always remember, as long as these activities are meaningful to you, they will be meaningful for the colleagues and superiors who care about you.

Insignificant Matters

As mentioned above, you should always speak about your accomplishments in definite terms and never minimize their importance for the sake of modesty.

Likewise, you should never refrain from divulging information about something you have achieved for the sake of shyness or because you think what you have achieved is insignificant or of minor importance.

Even the most insignificant accomplishments will be important to your colleagues and superiors because they will still give your colleagues and superiors the impression that you are a dynamic and active person and will help them to know you better.

Don't overdo it

As a final remark, remember that a sensible and balanced approach to self-promotion is all you need to get noticed internally and get ahead with your career progression. You don't need to over promote yourself or to over accomplish. Therefore, choose your activities carefully, and focus on doing them well.

Your aim is not to become visible all over the place but to be perceived by your colleagues and superiors as someone who is dynamic and successful in their personal life as well as in their professional one. Someone, in other words, who has the right personality and confidence to become a future leader of the firm.

7. The Benefits of Specialising

You may find that specializing in one or two niche areas within your general area of practice will help you progress your career significantly and achieve your partnership goals earlier for a number of reasons.

If you specialise, you will be able to add something extra to your practice group and your firm in general, and demonstrate your willingness to make an extra effort to further improve you competency and skills and your firm's reputation.

It will be easier for you to set yourself apart from the rest of your colleagues whose specialization and extra contribution to the firm will not be as apparent as yours. Accordingly, it will be easier for you to position yourself within your practice team and cover a clearly defined role within your firm.

As a consequence, your added value will be evident to your colleagues and the partners at your firm. Your will be perceived as a particularly valuable resource and recognised as someone willing to make an extra contribution to the success of your firm. Your value will be evident and this will greatly enhance your internal visibility and career prospects.

If you are fortunate enough to become the only expert in your chosen area of expertise, and this area is in high-demand, you will soon become indispensable to your firm. But even if, at least at the beginning, your chosen area of expertise is not particularly required, your extra efforts and initiative will still be noticed.

Specialising in one or two niche areas will also greatly enhance your business development potentials. It will help you focus your marketing efforts, since it is much easier to market a well-defined segment of the market rather than the whole of it.

Once you have clearly identified the type of clients who would most require your services and niche expertise, it will be much easier for you to approach those clients and market your services.

Over time you will hopefully build a small but growing following of clients, which will generate revenue for you and your firm. This following will make you become more independent and less reliant on your firm to provide you with work. This will give you confidence and bargaining power so far as your career advancement is concerned.

Investing your time into growing a small following of own clients will also give you the opportunity to practise your business development skills early in your career, skills that you will then be able to use to cultivate your firm's clients more effectively than the majority of your colleagues.

7.   Specialising: Practical Suggestions

Which specialisation

You should specialise in an area that is relatively new or underdeveloped but has significant growth potentials over the medium term.

The easiest way to find an area that has those attributes is to pay attention to recent developments in the law. The enactment of new legislation, in particular, has often created a sudden demand for legal services in areas that were previously unknown.

This has happened, for example, for data protection, freedom of information or financial crime. Before the relevant laws were enacted, none of these areas was recognised as a specialist practice area for lawyers in its own right.

Another effective way to find an area with growth potentials is to pay attention to changes in economic conditions and world trade. For example, it is easy to predict a surge in demand over the next 5 to 10 years for lawyers that are able to speak mandarin and deal with Chinese clients. How many lawyers, however, are committing themselves to study that language and get familiar with Chinese culture?

Keep yourself abreast of all recent market trends and, more importantly, develop the ability to predict changes in the marketplace. Once you have identified an up-and-coming trend, start working to gain a competitive advantage over your colleagues.

There will be more room for partners in practice areas that will be in high-demand, rather than in areas where there will be little work, and this is irrespective of whether the relevant areas are in high-demand at present.

You could become the most talented of lawyers but if there is not a sufficient market for your services, you will not be able to further your career much.

Similar considerations apply so far as internal demand is concerned. If you notice that your firm lacks resources in a particular area and believe there might be a market for your services there, you should try to specialise in that area so as to benefit from the relevant demand.

Your firm will greatly appreciate your efforts and, provided that you have been successful in meeting that demand, your firm will be willing to retain your services over the long term. You will have become too valuable to lose.

Specialising in an area that genuinely interests you will then give you even more professional satisfaction and it will be easier to strive for excellence if you are doing what you love. That said, even if you are not particularly passionate about the area of law you practise, you may still be able to become successful with commitment and hard work.

How to specialise

You do not have to qualify into a specialist department in order to become a specialist in a certain area, nor to practise it full time. In fact, most of the time, especially for up-and-coming areas, you will have to build your expertise from scratch.

If you are starting from scratch, you will have to develop a plan to acquire the knowledge required to work in that area and start gaining practical experience.

So far as the knowledge is concerned, you could start by reading everything you can get your hands on that relates to your chosen area. This includes trade publications, newspapers, magazines and the internet. You should also attend every relevant seminar, even if this will be on your own time and dime, and in particular every relevant trade association meeting.

You should then start to market your services to potential clients. Hopefully, by that time you will have gained an understanding of the type of client who might require your services and have made a few contacts.

Don't forget to also market yourself within your firm, especially if you work in a large firm or have access to a network of firms. Let everyone know that you are specialising in that area and ask them to refer any relevant work that might come into the firm to you. Write internal notes or give presentations if appropriate and seek every opportunity to raise awareness among your colleagues about your niche practice.

Depending on the type of specialisation you are seeking, you might even be able to market your services to other law firms and expand your network of contacts even more. Other law firms may become a precious source of referrals.

As long as a market exists for legal services in your chosen area of specialisation, there will certainly be clients who will be seeking your services. And as long as there will be clients who are seeking your services, there will be opportunities for partnership promotion.

8.   Performance Reviews

If you wish to become a partner at your firm, you have to gain a clear understanding, as early as possible, about your partnership potentials.

Most lawyers believe that if their firm is interested in promoting them to partnership, their firm will hint at it and be the first to discuss the topic when the right time comes. These lawyers believe that as long as they receive steady salary increases and are given opportunities for further professional growth, they are automatically on the track to become partners.

This belief can sometimes be incorrect though, and be the cause for great disappointment. Impressions can be misleading. In addition, it is often in a firm's interest to delay partnership considerations for as long as possible. Firms will not generally take initiatives unless forced to do so.

For all these reasons, it will be in your interest to seek feedback about your partnership potentials as early as possible in your career, and the best way to do this will be through your annual review. You should use your annual review to establish an open dialogue with your supervising partner about your career advancement and partnership potentials.

If you are a junior assistant and believe that it may be premature to discuss partnership prospects, you should at least ask explicitly your supervising partner whether you are on track with your firm's expectations for someone at your level of seniority. Once again, do not rely on your own impression of how things are going, but ask for an explicit feedback.

Good or bad, the feedback you will receive will be most precious to you. If it is positive feedback, you will know for sure that your career is progressing in accordance with your firm's and your own desires. If it is negative feedback, you will be pleased to have found out the truth sooner rather than later. If your career goal is to become a partner in private practice, you probably do not want to waste your time and energies working for a firm who is not prepared to offer you an opportunity for partnership.

9. Mentors

It will be easier for you to advance your career and become a partner in your firm if you are supported, advised and guided by a number of mentors who really care about you and your professional future.

With a bit of good judgment you will probably be able to make wise decisions about your present and future career by yourself. If, however, you are advised by someone who has more experience than you, chances are that you will be able to make even wiser choices, always provided that the person who advises you genuinely cares about you.

A mentor can advise you when you need advice, offer you support when you need it most and give you suggestions about all aspects of your work and professional development.

A number of mentors can provide even more. With a number of mentors to advise you, you will be able to call upon the right person at the right time. Each of your mentors provide their own contribution to your personal and professional development. In addition, with a number of mentors, you will also be able to seek assistance whenever you need it without over-burdening any one person.

You should therefore seek as many mentors as possible. Seek them both from within and outside your own firm. Anyone who you really trust and admire could become your mentor as long as they are willing to do so. Look for people you would like to emulate or who have some special expertise in the skills or areas in which you are interested.

Within your firm, it may prove particularly valuable to seek out mentors among the most senior people, irrespective of whether they are also the decision makers. The longer they have worked at your firm, the better they will know its secrets and culture and will be able to advise you correctly.

It does not matter whether you work in their department or not although, ideally, you may want your mentor to be someone who is not in a position to assess you from an employment point of view. Your mentor should be someone with whom you feel comfortable enough to honestly share questions and concerns. You may not feel entirely free to confide in your boss or openly discuss with them certain matters such as your career plans.

Mentors working at your firm will also be able to give you an insight into the balance of power within your firm and explain to you who the decision makers are, whom to seek out and whom not to cross. They will also be able to give you practical suggestions on how to become more visible within the firm and seek out the most interesting assignments.

If your mentors are powerful partners themselves, ensure that they will be there to sponsor you and support you when you need it. Ask them directly what they think you need to do to become a partner in your firm. Ask them for constant feedback on your progress and make sure that they will advocate for you when it is time for the partnership decision.

All mentors, whether they work at your firm or not, will generally be able to give you suggestions so far as business development is concerned and, especially if they are well established lawyers, introduce you to important contacts.

Mentors are an invaluable resource. Most people can count their memorable teachers, coaches and mentors on the fingers of one hand. So whenever you find someone whom you really admire, trust and respect, you should cherish them and make the most of them.

10. Be proactive

If you wish to become a partner, you will have to work on improving yourself every single moment of your life. You will have to commit yourself to seeking new challenges on a daily basis and proactively seeking personal and professional improvement opportunities if these are not automatically offered to you. You will have to constantly work on your personal and professional development and not waste any single minute of your time.

You should realise, if you have not realised it already, that the work habits you develop will make or break your career over the medium to long term. How you spend your spare time when in the office every day will play a crucial role in determining whether you will eventually be successful as a lawyer or not. The way you spend those ten, fifteen or thirty minutes of spare time you have every day will make a major difference over three, five or ten years' time.

If, for example, you are used to spending your spare time in the office studying new topics, reading legal articles and familiarising yourself with new documents and precedents, you will become a significantly better lawyer than if you are accustomed to spending your spare time browsing the internet, e-mailing friends or simply being lethargic. How you spend even five or ten minutes of your spare time per day will make a major difference over the medium to long term.

You should never waste any single minute of your time and instead use your time to improve yourself and seek new challenges and development opportunities. Listed below are a number of things you may be looking to do as part of your daily routine.

Volunteer for quality work

Whenever you find that you are not entirely occupied and have capacity to take on a new project, don't wait to be given the work from your superiors that they may decide to give you. Instead seek out the work that you would like to perform based on your own professional needs, so that you can gain experience in new areas, further your professional skills or even learn entirely new skills.

Remember that you are the only person responsible for your professional development. You should therefore take an active role and seek new professional challenges by yourself. You should never become complacent in your current job, especially if you are starting to feel unchallenged.

Ideally you should seek work that will enable you to develop new skills and stretch your existing skills. You should seek work that you have not performed before or is beyond your specialisation. Only this kind of work will push you out of your comfort zone and into an "unknown territory" offering you new difficulties and challenges.

This will be the only way for you to expand your skills and build your resilience and self-confidence. The more you stretch yourself and succeed, the more confident you will feel. And the more confident you feel, the more successful you will be. Be prepared, however, to make mistakes from time to time and don't be afraid to ask for help where required.

Needless to say, you should never refuse an assignment that is given to you by your superiors even if you feel that it might be beyond your current capabilities and specialisation. It would be a big mistake to refuse such assignment. There is no surer way to be crossed off the list for future opportunities than by refusing an offer.

Similar considerations apply to secondment opportunities and assignments to overseas offices. If your superiors have enough confidence in you to offer you these opportunities, you should have enough confidence to accept them.

Always be bold in taking on new projects and seek them actively if these are not offered to you.

Volunteer for leadership roles

Actively seek every opportunity to practise and develop your leadership skills and gain visibility within your firm. Join existing committees within your firm, volunteer for boards or even constitute new ones if you identify an opportunity to do so.

These opportunities will give you the chance to grow professionally as well as raising your profile and visibility within your firm. You will add value to and benefit your firm whilst creating new opportunities for career progression for yourself.

As mentioned, if you find that none of the existing committees and boards is interesting, you should not be afraid to try to set up a new one. This will show your colleagues and superiors that you are entrepreneurial, innovative and are not afraid to take and lead initiatives.

Seek business development opportunities

You should spend as much time as possible looking for conferences, seminars, trade exhibitions and other events that could give you the opportunity to make new contacts and develop your firm's business.

Once again, don't rely on anyone to provide you with business development opportunities and don't hesitate to pursue the opportunities you find by yourself on your own time and dime. Your returns could be extraordinary.

Seek learning opportunities

A proven way to advance in your career is to continually acquire new knowledge. Constantly seek new learning opportunities. Focus your efforts and try to become exceptionally knowledgeable on every topic that directly relates to your area of expertise or is otherwise connected to it.

Don't rely on your firm to provide you with learning opportunities and don't hesitate to further your education on your own time and dime. Remember that spending five or ten minutes per day in pursuing learning opportunities can make a major difference over the medium to long term.

* * *

If you consistently work on your personal and professional development, you will be on the right path to achieve great success and professional gratification. Your goals will soon become a reality.

11. Loyalty, Integrity & Perseverance

If you wish to become a partner, you have to understand the three key concepts of loyalty, integrity and perseverance.

Loyalty

It has been observed that, with a few exceptions, law firms tend to reward more lawyers who joined the firm at an early stage of their career rather than later hires.

Firm loyalty is in effect rewarded within the legal profession. Associates seem to have greater chances of becoming partners at a firm if they joined that firm at the beginning of their careers.

Especially if you are a fairly junior lawyer, you should therefore invest as much as you can in your current position rather than try to seek new opportunities elsewhere. Changing firm will probably give you an immediate monetary return in terms of a higher salary but this might come at a cost in terms of long-term career opportunities.

Follow the suggestions given earlier in this chapter about seeking feedback from your firm on your career prospects as early as possible. In principle, you should be looking to change firm only if you are told that there are no career opportunities for you there.

You should resist the temptation to change firm simply to get a higher salary, to join a busier environment or just for the sake of changing job. Likewise, don't be concerned about a short-term downturn in the economy or temporary lack of high profile instructions. Your career is a long-term investment.

However, if you are told that there are no career opportunities at your current firm, you should start considering your alternatives without delay. As already mentioned, time is a limited resource and should never be wasted under any circumstances.

Integrity

As you may already know, integrity is probably the single most important attribute of a successful lawyer. A lawyer who is less than completely honest and reliable, and who is not respected by his colleagues and clients without reservations, will not be around for very long.

Do what you say you will do and don't promise what you can't do, and you will be on the right path to achieving a long-term career. Time tends to reward integrity and honesty.

Perseverance

You will not be able to achieve your long-term career goals unless you believe in your capabilities and are confident that you can do it. People who believe they have the capacity to achieve their goals are far more likely to do so. Psychologists call this belief self-efficacy.

Likewise, you will not be able to achieve your goals unless you learn to be resilient and to persevere in the face of adversity.

Inevitably, there will be times during your career when you will experience difficulties, setbacks and obstacles and will feel discouraged and demoralised. You will not be able to survive those times without the necessary resilience and determination.

Whenever you experience difficulties, stay resolute in your values and goals and remain determined and self-disciplined in your efforts to achieve them. Believe you can achieve your goals, then analyse your problems and find a solution.

Don't ever succumb to feelings of helplessness. Instead, maintain your focus on your long term goals and find alternative ways to achieve them if required. Optimists see difficult times as learning opportunities and not as catastrophes with irrevocable effects.

In fact, optimism appears to be especially rare among lawyers, since so much of their work is about anticipating and preventing what could go wrong in a deal or court case. But even though pessimism may help you be more effective in practicing law, it will be an obstacle in your personal and professional life if you let it undermine your self-confidence.

You will only achieve all of your personal and professional goals if you truly believe in yourself and your capabilities.

CHAPTER 6 - BUSINESS DEVELOPMENT

1.　Importance of Business Development

It is probably fair to say that the main feature that characterises a truly successful lawyer is the ability to effectively market their services and develop and maintain a strong client following.

Business development skills are an essential tool in the armoury of a successful lawyer. Lawyers, like any other professional, must market their services effectively if they wish to be successful because a private practice, like any other business, is founded on sales. A private practice that fails to secure regular instructions from existing and new clients is bound to fail.

If you wish to become a truly successful lawyer, you should therefore realise the importance of marketing and selling your services effectively.

If you believe that marketing and selling is not necessarily part of the skill set of a lawyer, or that you did not go to law school to become a salesperson, think again. Otherwise, you will probably not remain in business for long, unless of course you work in-house and therefore are not required to generate business.

Even if you are a junior lawyer working in a large firm, don't make the mistake of thinking that generating work and securing client instructions is something for which only partners are responsible, something for which, in other words, you should not be concerned for the moment. You risk facing great difficulties later on in your career if you don't start practicing your marketing and selling skills from the very beginning.

It could be the case that, especially if you are working in a large City firm, business development will not be a condition precedent to partnership. Rainmaking potential, however, will certainly be. All firms, without exception, only promote to partnership associates who have the potential to enhance and expand relationships with existing clients and bring in new business.

Making a commitment to business development whilst still an associate will in addition be noted and appreciated by the partners at your firm, be taken into consideration at bonus time and increase your partnership potential.

Business development skills are even more important for lawyers who are already partners at their firm. Partners are generally well aware that if they wish to leave their firm and join a new firm, the first question a prospective new firm or recruitment agent will ask them the value of their client following.

Indeed, if you are no longer at the early stage of your career, you may have realised that only a strong client following will give you real control over your future, ensure that you keep your position within your firm, are able to move to another firm or establish your own practice if you wish to do so.

In other words, excellent work and technical skills will not guarantee your long-term success in the legal profession unless they are accompanied by effective marketing and selling skills. Whilst technically excellent lawyers are still rewarded and appreciated for their work, they are rarely rewarded as handsomely as rainmakers and, as mentioned, are not in control of their future.

Despite all this, lawyers generally receive very little training in marketing and selling. So when the time comes to take responsibility for generating new business for their firm, most lawyers find the relevant task daunting, if not scary, and feel awkward in their marketing and selling efforts.

These lawyers, in particular, still consider marketing and selling as being very uncomfortable endeavours, unpleasant, embarrassing, even repugnant and certainly anything but professional.

If you are part of this group of lawyers, you may wish to reconsider your views on these subjects and start looking at marketing and selling as something which constitutes an integral part of being a lawyer in a private practice, something that, with the right education and training, will become a pleasant and comfortable way to achieve professional success and job security. Once again, developing good business development skills is the best career insurance you can have as a lawyer.

The following pages will introduce you to the fundamentals of marketing and selling. Whilst not purporting to be comprehensive, these sections will hopefully enhance your understanding of those topics and provide an introduction to the most important marketing and selling techniques.

Once again, it will be up to you to further educate yourself on these topics if you wish to do so, for example by reading specialist books or attending classes or workshops. A list of the articles and books which have informed the following sections, and which may be used for further reading, is provided in the bibliography at the end of this book.

2. Client Analysis

One of the most effective ways for you to understand where you are in the marketing cycle and, more importantly, in which direction you should point your marketing efforts, is to perform a detailed analysis of your current client base. The aim of this analysis is to gain a better insight as to who your clients are and where they came from.

Look at your existing clients and identify what they have in common. Look at their size, their industry sector, management structure and operations. If your clients are large corporations, ask yourself whether you receive instructions from the management or legal counsel.

Look at how many clients you have and how the total revenues are distributed among them. Usually, in accordance with the Pareto principle of economic distribution, you will find that approximately eighty percent of your revenues are generated by twenty percent of your clients. If you can, divide your clients into at least three different revenue ranges.

Then look at the profitability of each client. Not all instructions generate the same amount of profit. Once again, you might want to divide your clients into at least three different profitability ranges, high, middle and low profitability.

Lastly, look at the specific type of work you provide to those clients and identify those three or four areas of work that are most required by your clients as a whole.

After you have spent time classifying your client base, you can then start interpreting the relevant data. Looking at the data, you should begin to see a picture forming. Try to identify patterns and common threads, detect problem areas and find areas for improvement or further development.

For example, are the clients who generate the most revenue also generating the most profit? If not, would it not make more sense to shift your focus from these clients to your other more profitable clients and try to win more work from them?

Do certain areas of work expose you to particular risks so far as professional liability is concerned? If so, does the level of profitability of the relevant work provide a good reason for continuing to deal with those areas?

Look then at where your clients came from and why they use your services. Identify the channels through which the majority of your clients came to you and, once again, make sure that you spend some time identifying patterns and looking for areas of further expansion.

You may find, for example, that a significant number of clients came to you through a certain network of referrals. In this case, you should clearly consider investing more time into cultivating that network. Or if you find that a number of profitable clients came to you following a presentation you gave at a trade association, you should consider getting even more involved in that association, for example, by writing articles in their newsletter or trade magazine.

It is important that you clearly understand the reasons your clients use your services as opposed to those of one of your competitors. If you wish to really understand where you are in your marketing cycle, it is imperative that you understand the motivations of your clients in choosing you.

Interview your clients for these purposes and do not try to guess their reasons or dismiss this exercise by thinking that their motivations might be obvious. In order to assess your marketing potential, it is imperative that you understand precisely that motivates your clients since even the most trivial reasons might constitute the starting point for defining a marketing plan.

If for example you find that most of your clients instruct you because you are a close friend of theirs, there will be probably very little point in you working to promote your specialist expertise through publications or speeches. Your time would be better invested into networking and building personal relationships with potential clients.

By contrast, if you find that most of your clients are referred to you by the head of your department or firm, your time would be probably best spent investing in your relationship with them to ensure continued referrals rather than trying to open up new channels of your own.

Once again, identify patterns and common threads and find areas for development.

3.   Business Development Plan

After having considered your current client base, you should have acquired a better idea of which kind of clients you wish to pursue more and which channels you should use. You should then devise a detailed business development plan.

Developing your own individual marketing plan will enable you to make optimal use of your time and energy, and avoid getting sidetracked by false opportunities that don't fit with your priorities.

Make sure that your plan is broken down into small action steps that you can easily accomplish and is realistic in term of time commitment. Ideally, you should use one or more of the marketing tools that are presented in the following pages. Write down your plan as a bullet point action plan.

Ensure that your plan is tailored at targeting no more than one or two groups of clients (or client segments) so that your marketing efforts do not get diluted. You will always be able to market your services to additional segments of the market at a later stage.

Remember the suggestions given previously in this book about the need to specialise as much as possible. Clients generally feel that they will get a greater value for their money by seeking specialist advice rather than spending less money for similar expertise from a generalist. Accordingly, they will be willing to pay a premium for your expertise.

Your chosen client niche must primarily provide an opportunity for growth or at least a guarantee of sustainable earnings for a number of years, and whether you find the relevant sector interesting or not is of secondary importance.

As mentioned, a genuine enthusiasm, interest and passion for the work you are seeking will generally help you market your services in your chosen sector but are not, however, strictly required and you will still be able to succeed with the right determination and skill.

Your business development plan does not have to fit necessarily within your firm's overall plan, as long as you are confident that you will be able to generate clients that provide at least the same level of profitability provided by your firm's existing clients. Your fellow partners will generally not mind having you develop your own niche within the firm as long as general profitability is safeguarded. They will rather compliment you for your initiatives and entrepreneurship.

As mentioned, as a future or present partner, you should think and act with your own head and not your firm's. If you wish to become a successful lawyer, you have to grow a business owner's mentality and not that of an employee.

4. Marketing Tools

There are a number of traditional marketing tools which you should consider using as part of your marketing activities. These tools are writing and publishing, giving presentations and public speeches and networking. This section will deal with the first two while a later section of this book will deal with networking.

Remember, when planning your marketing activities, that the principal purpose of your endeavours is to get noticed by prospective clients within your chosen market. You should become more visible and credible in the eyes of your prospective clients, and appear to them as *the* expert to go to in case of need.

Your marketing activities should also be aimed at generating new client contacts and leads. Sometimes appearing as *the* expert in your chosen field will not be sufficient to secure instructions from new clients unless you have also been able to establish direct contact with them. Make sure that, whenever you find a new lead, you follow up, even briefly, by sending a personal letter of introduction or arranging a meeting for lunch or coffee.

Once you have commenced your marketing activities, keep an accurate record of all your endeavours. As soon as you have gathered a meaningful amount of data, assess which of the activities you carried out produced the best results in terms of leads generated and new client contacts. Going forward, you may want to concentrate your efforts by doing more of these most fruitful activities.

By contrast, you should reconsider your entire marketing plan if none of your marketing activities has produced the desired results. If for example your entire marketing plan consisted of networking activities, and these have proved wholly unsuccessful, you should start considering shifting your focus towards other forms of marketing such as writing an article or giving a speech.

At the same time, make sure that you give yourself enough time before deciding which activities worked and which didn't. Every marketing activity takes some time to come to fruition so you should not give up unless, for example, you have been carrying out the relevant activity continuously for at least six months.

In effect, if you have carried out marketing activities in the past, and have kept an accurate record of those activities, you should be able to identify how long it typically takes for a certain activity to generate results. In all these cases, you should never give up the relevant activity unless the required time has passed.

For example, if you know from past experiences that it typically takes one year of continuous attendances for you to become known among the members of a certain club or organisation, you should not critically assess you plan within this period. Likewise, if you know that you have to publish at least three articles in a certain trade magazine before starting to receive queries from potential clients, you should not give up publishing articles in that magazine until you have published at least the three requisite articles.

Whatever your activity, keep an accurate record of it and persevere until, after you have spent the optimal number of hours or money pursuing it, you can conclude that that activity has not generated the desired results and should therefore be discontinued.

Writing and publishing

Writing and publishing are powerful ways of reaching potential clients and developing credibility within your chosen market. The author of a publication on a technical subject is always perceived to be an expert in the relevant subject, whether or not that is actually true. In addition, written publications leave tangible records that will remain forever available to you and, subject to the necessary updates, may be used for future marketing activities.

There are two main types of writing and publishing that you could use: newsletters and articles in magazines or other publications.

Both of these means will give you the opportunity to gain exposure as an expert within your target audience whilst retaining complete control over the publication. A newsletter or a regular feature within a third party publication, in particular, will allow you to stay in contact with your clients on a frequent and regular basis.

If your firm does not already send a newsletter to its clients, you may wish to consider starting one. With desktop publishing applications, preparing, printing and distributing a professional-looking newsletter has become a fairly inexpensive and easily manageable process.

Before starting a newsletter, however, carefully assess the time commitments it will require and make sure that, even during busy periods, the preparation of the newsletter will not become a burden or conflict with your work commitments. Similar considerations apply so far as publishing a regular feature in third party magazines or other publications is concerned.

That said, it is fair to say that among all marketing tools, writing regular articles or newsletters will give you the most exposure to potential clients and help you build tremendous credibility.

If you are planning to publish an article, make sure that it is published in a magazine or other publication that is likely to be read by potential clients (and not only other lawyers).

Public speaking

Public speaking is another effective way of developing credibility within your chosen market and giving potential clients the impression that you are an expert in the subject-matter concerned, whether or not that is actually true. As such, it is generally regarded as an effective marketing tool for lawyers.

Public speaking can take the form of a speech, a seminar or a workshop, depending on the amount of audience participation and length. Whilst a speech will generally use the least amount of audience participation and be limited in time, a workshop will have the most audience involvement and last much longer. A seminar will be somewhere in between.

Needless to say, the more the audience participates and the greater the length of the presentation, the more you will have to prepare yourself and the higher level of knowledge on the subject you will have to show your audience.

Be aware that public speaking is generally a less effective marketing tool than writing and publishing, so far as the generation of new leads is concerned. Writing and publishing can reach a wider audience than public speaking in terms of numbers. In addition, reading an article creates far less inconvenience than having to attend a seminar or workshop.

If you are considering preparing a speech, seminar or workshop, also bear in mind the risks associated with the fact that you will not be in control of your audience. Attendees might ask you questions which you are not prepared or willing to answer.

The Public Speaking Chapter of this book contains a number of suggestions that will help you prepare and deliver an effective presentation and improve your public speaking skills.

Leverage your marketing activities

As a final remark on the topics of writing, publishing and public speaking, remember that a single project can be recycled into a number of different activities and that the slides of a presentation can, with a little extra effort, become a short article. A short article, or a collection of short articles, can in turn become a brochure and, perhaps, even a brief booklet or guide.

Whatever you do, leverage your marketing efforts as much as you can and get the maximum usage out of the work you have done.

5.   Networking

Networking, at least in its traditional sense, is arguably the most overrated business development activity a lawyer can possibly undertake. Yet it still appears to be the most practised, especially by those lawyers who are not willing to put in the extra effort required to pursue more effective marketing activities like writing and publishing or public speaking.

You too have probably attended business or other similar events in the past with a view to meeting potential clients or getting new leads, only to be eventually disappointed by your results. In effect, statistics suggest that less than one in fifteen people met at the so called networking events has concrete potential of generating new business.

That said, if you wish to include an element of networking within your marketing activities, here are a number of suggestions that will help you improve your success rate.

Where to network

Avoid circulating at traditional business events such as industry gatherings, conferences and any other events where other lawyers are likely to be present. As a rule of thumb, the more lawyers you find at a networking event, the less probable it is that the people attending that event could become a source of work.

Instead, search for events, seminars and conferences that, whilst still having a business or professional connotation, relate to industries that do not have any obvious connection with the legal industry.

For example, if you are a property lawyer, you may find more useful to attend a conference primarily aimed at economists on the status of the UK economy than a gathering organised by a trade association of property developers. Chances are that you will be a more curious and interesting presence at the former event rather than the latter, with the result that people at the former event will be more interested to know about you and your services.

Any property developer you might meet at the gathering of property developers, by contrast, will know from the time they meet you that you are there primarily to sell your services and will therefore be less interested in knowing you. In fact, chances are that by the time you get to know them they have already spoken to dozen of other property lawyers.

Try to attend events that do not have any business connotation at all and instead are social in nature, like book clubs meetings, artistic or musical events, painting exhibitions, antiques fairs, food or wine tasting and so on, as long as, of course, you might meet people who might become potential clients there.

You will have better chances to make useful contacts at these events than at traditional networking events because all the attendees will be relaxed and willing to engage in interesting conversation with you. They will probably not be under time pressure nor feel required to act in a formal, businesslike manner. These events will also constitute an opportunity for personal growth for you.

How to create and maintain a network

Don't make the mistake of thinking that networking is essentially a matter of knowing as many people as possible and collecting a large number of business cards.

Shaking someone's hand and talking briefly at a meeting, following-up afterwards with a phoney "it was nice to meet you-we should stay in touch" kind of e-mail and then failing to build a meaningful and mutually beneficial relationship with the relevant person will not take you anywhere.

If you really wish to become a successful networker, you should work on building few sincere, significant relationships with people who you genuinely like and trust. Whether these relationships will evolve into friendship or business relationships is irrelevant. What is really important is that the relationships you build are genuine and, over time, become more and more meaningful.

Only at that stage will the people in your network start to keep you in mind for business opportunities and referrals.

Networking, in other words, is not a game of numbers. Investing your time and money into building few but meaningful relationships will give you a much better return in terms of marketing your services and generating new business than having a large number of meaningless contacts.

Time commitment

If you decide to incorporate networking activities within your marketing plan, you will have to devote substantial time (and money) to the pursuit of those activities.

If seriously pursued as a marketing activity, networking tends to be more time consuming than writing and publishing or public speaking. You will spend a considerable number of hours searching for suitable events, participating at those events, following-up with the people you have met and meeting them from time to time.

In addition, networking will have far more uncertain and less tangible results than most of the other marketing activities considered in this chapter, at least in the short term.

In light of all the above considerations, you may wish to very carefully consider whether to include networking activities in your marketing strategy.

6. Empathy

You will be surprised about the high number of qualified leads that an effective marketing plan will generate for you, especially if you have never planned your marketing activities before.

Generating a large number of responses, however, will be of little value if you are not able to convert the leads generated into actual business, that is to say, if you are not able to effectively sell your services to potential clients.

There are a number of concepts and techniques that could dramatically improve your ability to sell your services effectively to the new leads. Since this book, however, does not offer the opportunity to deal with all those concepts and techniques, this section will only focus on what is arguably the most important selling concept of all, the concept of empathy.

Empathy (sometimes referred to as "emotional intelligence") can be defined as the ability to read and understand another person's thoughts and feelings with a view to start seeing things from their perspective. Empathy is the ability to understand another person's point of view in a common situation, and understand the motivations, concerns, feelings and ambitions of the other person.

You are showing empathy when you take the time to put yourself in someone else's shoes and make a sincere and unbiased effort to understand why that person behaves the way they do. You free yourself from judgment in order to become compassionate and understanding.

If you wish to win new clients and retain your existing clients, you have to learn how to show empathy towards the personal and business needs of your clients and start looking at your relationship with those clients from the client's (and not the lawyer's) perspective. You have, in other words, to start living the whole client-lawyer experience from your client's point of view.

This is particularly important for potential clients whom you have just met. Unless they perceive that you are on the same wavelength as them and that you experience what they are experiencing, they will not open up to you, begin to trust you or eventually hire your services.

If you wish to establish rapport with new clients, you have to show them that you fully appreciate the emotional situation which they are in, from a human perspective even before a business one, and understand their motivations and concerns. If you fail to align yourself with your client, you will generally not be able to satisfy your clients' needs in full.

If, for example, you are advising the director of a company on a proposed deal, you should never forget when talking to that person that at stake is not the successful completion of the deal per se but the financial security and career prospects of that director.

If you are able to show them that you really understand the issues at stake and can be compassionate with them, chances are that you will build a rapport so strong that your clients will never consider hiring any other lawyer and will also be forgiving if you commit a mistake or do not perform at your best in that situation.

The above considerations apply whatever area of law you practise and type of client you serve. More often than not, the issues at stake are not what they seem to be and the real issues are often to be found at a more deep and meaningful personal level.

If you realise this fundamental concept, you will be on your way to winning and retaining considerably more instructions than the majority of your competitors. A lawyer who can really empathize with prospects or clients will always succeed at getting their business, loyalty and referrals.

7.   Client Interview: Practical Suggestions

The suggestions contained in the communication sections of this book will be particularly useful when you are invited by a prospective client to pitch for work. Whether you have been invited to make a formal pitch or to discuss informally possible instructions, you should always bear in mind the importance of focusing your attention on how you will be perceived by your prospective client.

The following suggestions will further help you succeed at client interviews.

Believe you can win the instructions

A discreet number of lawyers pitching for work often don't expect to win the instructions and are discouraged even before starting their pitch. These lawyers have failed their pitches so many times in the past that they are actually surprised when they succeed.

These lawyers are able to provide a large number of reasons for which their pitch is bound to fail even before it started, as if they are trying to persuade themselves that nobody would ever hire their services. According to these lawyers, clients don't ever change legal advisers.

Don't be like these lawyers. This kind of attitude can only attract negativity and failure. If you wish to succeed when pitching for work, you have to truly believe, without any reservation whatsoever, and despite all the odds, that you are going to succeed.

Assume that you are going to win the pitch. Be confident that, once you get into your presentation, your prospective client will not be able to say no. Visualise your success, if this can help you, and imagine that you have won your pitch even before you have actually started.

Believe that you are the best lawyer of your kind and that you would do a terrific job for this client. Whatever your inspiration, just be confident that you are going to succeed. Otherwise, you are probably better off refraining from pitching at all.

Similar considerations apply so far as marketing is concerned. If you believe that clients don't ever change legal advisers, and that accordingly your marketing activities will not generate the desired outcome, you are probably better off refraining from doing any marketing at all.

Manage Your Emotions

When pitching for work with a new client, the ability to manage your emotions and anxiety will be paramount. Throughout your presentation, you should constantly monitor yourself, pay attention to your feelings and your body language and manage all these elements effectively.

It will be particularly important that you maintain a body language that stresses professionalism and performance. As in any other situation, you should ensure that, if nothing else, you body language transmits a message of confidence and calmness.

Especially when meeting a new client, you will be judged as soon as you arrive at their offices. If you feel nervous, make sure that you arrive at the appointment early so that you can use the extra time to relax and concentrate on your impending presentation. If you are asked to wait in a waiting area, avoid opening your briefcase to review your notes and your agenda. Instead, glance at the magazines and newspapers available in the waiting area.

When you are informed that your prospective client is ready to see you, enter their office with confidence and don't hesitate by, for example, feebly knocking at their door, or opening it and peeking in. These behaviours might be interpreted as lack of confidence on your part. Instead, knock at the door with decision and walk straight towards your host when you enter the room. Then greet your host with a firm handshake and a sincere smile, and let your conversation begin.

Whilst trying to manage your emotions and anxiety, be careful not to exaggerate your body language. You risk, otherwise, showing over-confidence, arrogance and self- importance. Instead, let your host set the tone of the interview and match their behaviour, body language and voice tone as much as you can.

Remember that succeeding at a client interview and getting the instructions is not only about having the right combination of relevant experience, skills and personal attributes. It is also about how you relate to your potential client and establish rapport with them at your first meeting.

Practise Active Listening

The most effective way to succeed at client interviews is to practise active listening. Active listening is the ability to engage someone in conversation by simply asking questions and listening carefully to the answers, as opposed to doing all the talking yourself.

It has been suggested that when a client is considering hiring a lawyer, or any other professional for that matters, they are not so much interested in the lawyer's technical capabilities, which are to a large extent given for granted, as to the lawyer's ability to listen to and understand the client's requirements and unique motivations.

When discussing possible instructions, your main concern should not be making sure that you show your client that you have the right expertise and capabilities to do the job effectively. Your main concern should rather be showing your client sufficient concern about their situation and needs, and asking as many questions as possible.

As a rule of thumb, the more questions you ask a potential client at a client interview, the more chance you have of winning the relevant instructions. Remember that it's all about the client and their concern and not about you, and that, whenever you are in a room with a potential or existing client, you are the least important person in the room.

Even if you should be telling your client what to do and how to best approach their situation, you should pretend that *they* are the experts and, accordingly, ask them how *they* think their problem could be resolved, what *they* think the possible solutions are and what *they* think the best solutions is.

It will be easy for you to realise the importance of active listening if you consider the following example. Imagine that you are looking for a babysitter to take care of your children while you are at work.

The first potential babysitter tells you about what kind of a person *she* is, how often *she* does babysitting, how scrupulous *she* is to ensure that the children are taken care of and how *she* usually addresses their needs while the children's parents are away.

The second potential babysitter asks you instead what *you* are looking for in a babysitter, what concerns *you* have about leaving your child while you are at work, how *you* take care of your children when you are there and what *you* would like her to do to address the needs of your children while you are away.

Assuming both babysitters have equal training and experience, whom would you hire?

Shift the focus from you to your prospective client, practise active listening, and you will significantly increase your success when pitching for work. Asking as many questions as possible will also help you prevent any misunderstanding, clarify ambiguity and manage any unrealistic expectations you prospective client might have.

Show enthusiasm and ask for their business

Showing enthusiasm and exhibiting a genuine interest in establishing a working relationship with a potential client will significantly increase your chances of success. As you might already know, enthusiasm is contagious. Accordingly, it is more difficult to say no to someone who is really enthusiastic about a work opportunity than someone who lacks enthusiasm and energy.

Also, let the client know that you would like to work for them and don't be afraid to ask explicitly for their business. Don't let your shyness or fear stop you. You potential client will feel better knowing that their instructions are important to you because this will reassure them that you will give them the attention and care they deserve.

Even after you have secured your instructions, show enthusiasm and appreciation to your client as if they were your only client.

Your Closing Argument

Making a good last impression at a client interview will be almost as important as making a good first impression. A strong finish will leave a lasting impression on your client's mind that will work to your benefit even after you have left your client's office.

Just as you did when you entered your client's office, look your host in the eye, smile, and shake their hand firmly. Thank them for taking the time to meet with you and let them know, again, that you look forward to working for them.

The sale begins after the sale

There is an old adage among sales and marketing professionals that says "the sale begins after the sale". This adage applies to the sale of legal services as well as any other service.

Winning the instructions from a new client will only be the beginning of the story. Your win will be short-lived if you fail to retain your new client and establish a long-term relationship with them which will provide you with repeat business and referrals.

As you are probably aware, this will only be possible if you provide your new client with a truly outstanding service and excellent client care. Only on this basis will you receive repeat business and referrals. Otherwise, you will have to start all over again.

Receiving repeat business from an existing client is far easier than winning instructions from a new client and that repeat business and referrals, over the long term, is the only way you can establish a strong client base which, hopefully, will accompany and support you for the rest of your career.

Your reputation, your integrity and your ability to provide your clients with a truly outstanding service will be key to achieving success as a lawyer over the long term.

8. Job Interviews

The suggestions provided in the above sections, in particular section 6 (Empathy) and section 7 (Client Interview: Practical Suggestions), are applicable also if you are being interviewed for a job, at any level.

Interviewing is about selling yourself and therefore, like in any selling situation, the focus should not be on you (and what *you* have to offer) but on the buyer, in this case your prospective employer, and what *they* are looking for. Remember the baby sitter example given before.

Step into the interviewer's shoes and ask early in the interview: "What are you looking for in the person you wish to hire?", "What is the most important attribute that the person you are looking to hire should have?" and "What would be my first priorities on the job?". The earlier you ask these questions, the sooner you will build rapport with the interviewer.

Listen carefully to the answers you are given and make sure that your subsequent answers are tailored to the employer's priorities. Tell the interviewer that, based on what you have been told, you believe you are a suitable match and then ask the interviewer whether they have any concerns about your ability to do the job. This will be particularly powerful and will give you an opportunity to address during the interview any concerns or doubts the interviewer might have.

If you follow the above suggestions, and have armed yourself with the necessary dose of preparation and confidence, you will perform at the interview fantastically well.

CHAPTER 7 - DELEGATION

1. Importance of Delegation

Learning to delegate effectively will be essential to your success as a lawyer. Without the ability to delegate efficiently to your colleagues, assistants and support staff, you will not be able to run your practice in a successful and profitable fashion.

The more senior a lawyer you are, the more you will need to use delegation skills. Only by delegating tasks effectively, will you be able to run a number of different projects at the same time, become more productive in your daily work and, more importantly, free up valuable time to dedicate yourself to more strategic issues and pursue business development opportunities.

By delegating effectively, you will also be less likely to stagnate in work of the same type and standard and, as a consequence, you will be able to get involved in new tasks and projects that interest you.

The same considerations apply even if you are a junior lawyer. By learning the basics of delegation and practising the relevant skill as much as you can, you will free up valuable time to focus on your ongoing professional development and prepare yourself for the time when you will be leading your own team of lawyers.

Delegation will also provide you with a number of other benefits, including improved performance of your team as a whole, improved competence of the members of your team and improved speed and confidence in the more junior members. All this will translate, as you may expect, into a better and more cost effective service for your clients and general client satisfaction.

Delegating effectively, however, can be also one of the most challenging tasks for a lawyer. The main reason for this is that lawyers are generally taught at an early stage in their career that self-reliance and independence are two major factors in determining the success of a lawyer.

Whilst this may be true at the beginning of a lawyer's career, it becomes less and less true the more senior a lawyer becomes. Partners, in particulars, would not be able to run their practice at all without the daily support of their assistants and support staff.

Keep this in mind if you are about to be appointed, or have recently been appointed, to a senior position within your firm. Unless you relinquish your individual contributor mindset, you will not be able to lead your team effectively and be successful in your new role. In sharp contrast with what you were taught at the beginning of your career, your job is now to get the work done through others and not do the work by yourself.

This might be challenging at first but, over time, with the necessary training and practice, you will soon start enjoying the benefits that being able to delegate work will provide to you.

As mentioned, learning to delegate effectively will be essential to your success as a lawyer. So commit yourself to delegate as much work as you can from now on so that you free up valuable time to focus on what is most important to you.

2. Overcoming Resistance

As mentioned in the previous section, there are a number of psychological barriers that you have to overcome if you wish to learn to delegate effectively.

Desire to remain comfortable in your current role

Certain lawyers resist delegation because they do not feel comfortable with it. Since they are not accustomed to delegating work, they prefer to carry on doing their work directly as they have always done.

Do not let your past work habits stop you from delegating. The more senior you become, the less you will be able to carry on doing your work directly as you have always done. Sooner than you might expect, delegation may become a necessity and not an option.

Therefore, start practicing delegation as soon as you are given an opportunity, even if initially you feel uncomfortable with it. In your work as well as in your life, you should always stretch yourself, be open to learning and be flexible and adaptable in every situation.

The belief that you can do a better and quicker job yourself

This is a very common reason for lawyers to resist delegation. Of course none of your team members will be able to do the job as well and as fast as you.

Remember, however, that you may not be able to do the job all by yourself because you have more important tasks to carry out. And that perhaps, if you trust others to be capable of producing a good piece of work, you will still accomplish a more than satisfactory result in a very cost-effective way.

Concern that you may appear less efficient and willing to work hard

This is another very common reason for lawyers to resist delegation and is based on the idea that the real value of a lawyer is shown by their ability to do their work all by themselves and not through others.

This idea is without foundation. Leadership and delegation skills are as valuable for a lawyer as self-reliance and independence. Learn therefore to appreciate and value your leadership skills as you value your ability to do work on your own.

Do not make the mistake of thinking that, because it is not billable, the time you spend coaching members of your team is not well invested. Although your firm may not compensate you directly for this time, your ultimate success, among other things, will be dependent on your ability to delegate work effectively and be a good leader for your team members.

Fear of losing control

The fear of losing control over how work is done and the inability to fully check its accuracy are by far the most common reasons for lawyers to resist delegation. Most lawyers cannot overcome the fear that a subordinate might make mistakes and put at risk the successful completion of a whole project. The whole idea of losing control and letting go is generally very anxiety-producing for lawyers.

When you find yourself having this concern, remind yourself that you may simply not be able in the circumstances to do all the work by yourself and that, in any case, delegating does not mean that you will abdicate control over the final product. You will always have a chance to review the work done by your team members before it is sent to the client.

Over time, you may even find that if you train your team members effectively they will become able to perform the work with the same diligence that you would have used. This will be most empowering and should give you great comfort.

It has also been suggested that a lawyer who has learned to delegate effectively will actually gain a better control over their practice by working through others rather than doing all the work by themselves.

This is not to say that by delegating you will not take a risk that the person you delegate to might make a mistake. Remember, however, that people learn from mistakes and that, accordingly, your team members will be able to do a better job the next time. Chances are that you too have learned valuable lessons from your past mistakes.

Therefore make use of delegation as much as you can and resist the temptation of doing all the work by yourself. By following the suggestions given in the following sections, you will significantly improve your delegation skills and accordingly reduce the risks associated with delegation.

3.   Motivation

Before dealing with the practical aspects of delegation, it is essential that you understand that no delegation will ever be possible if the people to whom you delegate are not willing to help you in your project and sufficiently motivated to give you their support.

Unless the people to whom you delegate are willing to support you and work towards your goals, you won't be able to succeed at getting commitment, quality work and productivity from them, and this irrespective of how good your delegating skills are.

Before focusing on learning the practical aspects of delegation, you should therefore learn how to motivate people. This means being able to understand why people do what they do and how you can motivate them to do what you want them to do.

There are a number of books and publications on motivation, some of which are listed in the bibliography and reading list at the end of this book. You may want to read one or more of those books and publications if you wish to gain a deeper understanding of motivational theory.

For the purposes of this book, however, it is sufficient that you realise that each person is motivated by different things and that, unless you take the time to consider what motivates each individual member of your team, you won't be able to make the most of them so far as their performance is concerned.

Take the time to consider each individual member of your team and ask yourself what motivates them the most. Some of your team members, for example, might be motivated by a desire for recognition and appreciation, others by a desire for responsibility and career advancement, others by a desire for ongoing professional development and personal growth, others by a desire for some flexibility in their work schedule and others by a simple desire for more money.

Once you have identified what motivates each of your team members, you will be able to dispense in the right doses what is most desired by them. You may find that a "stick and carrot" approach will be particularly helpful in this respect, and that by giving or threatening to withdraw, depending on the circumstances, what is most desired by each of your team members, you will be able to achieve your goals.

You should constantly praise those team members who are most motivated by a desire for recognition and appreciation before clients and colleagues, assign additional functions to those who are motivated by a desire for responsibility and career advancement, offer more opportunities for training to those who are motivated by a desire for ongoing professional development (typically the most junior lawyers) and dispense regular performance related bonuses to those who are motivated by money.

Equally importantly, you should not give someone something that will not satisfy their desires in full, like giving monetary rewards to someone who is motivated by a desire for some flexibility in their work schedule, or give increased training opportunities to someone who is driven by a desire for more money.

Whenever you are in doubt about what really motivates your team members, don't be afraid to ask. As mentioned, it will be impossible to get commitment from your team unless you understand exactly what are the goals, attitudes and concerns of each of your team members. If you are unsure, you should not be afraid to ask your team members directly what motivates them and how you can ensure their full cooperation and commitment going forward.

If you follow the above suggestions, you will create an environment in which self-motivation can flourish and you will soon find yourself surrounded by a team who is constantly willing to give you all their support and work hard for your own (and their own) success.

4. Project Management & Preparation

As you may already know, when you are in charge of a project, irrespective of its complexity, you should avoid the tendency to start working immediately and should instead take the time to plan which activities are required for its successful completion and how those activities should be implemented.

Before anything else, you should take the time to carefully consider the whole project from start to finish, define the project's objectives and all necessary activities. Take the time to understand where you are and what you wish to accomplish and then write an outline, list or sketch of all the activities and tasks that need to be completed in order to achieve successful completion of the whole project.

Using a well-known technique among project management experts, visualise in your mind the desired outcome of the project and then work your way backwards to identify which steps need to be taken to achieve that desired outcome.

Ensure that you gain a very clear picture of what each task entails and what exactly is required for its successful completion. Break large tasks into manageable pieces and plan thoroughly how to achieve them. Once again, visualise in your mind what the finished task or product should look like.

You should then ask yourself which of the tasks you have identified can be delegated to other people and which, by contrast, you should do by yourself. As mentioned, avoid the tendency to do too many things by yourself and instead try to delegate tasks as much as you can. As a rule of thumb, you should try to delegate every activity that can be done by others and keep for yourself only those activities that only you can do.

Be careful, however, not to overdo it and, above all, refrain from delegating tasks simply because you find those tasks particularly difficult, annoying or tedious. The person to whom you delegate those tasks will realise it and will not appreciate your behaviour. Even more so if they suspect that the only reason you have delegated the task to them is that you are not able to complete it by yourself.

Once you have identified which tasks you should delegate, you can then consider which member of your team would be most suitable to deal with each task.

Consider what skills and capabilities are required to successfully complete each task and compare the required skills with the current level of competency of your team members. Resist the temptation of delegating a task to someone that you already know would be able to easily deal with the relevant task and instead give the task to someone who may not be entirely ready to deal with it.

The person to whom you delegate the task will appreciate the trust and confidence you are giving them and feel motivated to work hard towards the successful completion of the task. They will feel motivated by the sense that they are acquiring a new skill and will do their best to meet your expectations in full.

As a consequence, they will be willing to stretch themselves and deliver an excellent job. Most people, in effect, develop by being stretched and if you expect them to succeed, they probably will.

Be careful however not to assign a task to someone whose skills fall far short of what is required to effectively complete the task. Asking them to complete a task that is too far beyond their present capabilities will simply set them up for failure and demoralise them.

Likewise, avoid giving a task to someone who is not entirely ready to take it on if you have little time to train them about how to get the task done because of time restraints. In these circumstances, you should assign a task only if you are entirely confident that the person to whom you assign the task can complete it with a minimum of direction.

To preserve motivation among your team members, try to distribute the more mundane and tedious tasks as evenly as possible. When delegating a tedious task, be careful to delegate not only the performance of the task but also its ownership and encourage the person to whom you delegate the task to change, develop or upgrade the product concerned if desirable.

Remember always to check the existing workload of the person to whom you are proposing to delegate a task beforehand, so that the person concerned is not overwhelmed. Your goal is to optimise resources and not burn them out. At the same time, when you do assign a task to someone, make sure that they will allocate the time required to the task.

Delegate in time and decide as early as possible on who should be dealing with what. It will be your responsibility to allow the person to whom you delegate a task sufficient time for the relevant task to be carried out.

Then write down a list of the names of the people to whom you are delegating work with an indication of what work was given out and when it is due in. This will be your job-tracking sheet.

5.   Giving Instructions

There are a number of steps that you should follow to ensure that you communicate clearly with your team members when you are instructing them.

Explain the background

Your team members will contribute most effectively if you take the time to explain to them the background of the instructions and how the delegated task will fit in the big picture and why it needs to be accomplished.

This will ensure a greater understanding of the instructions and, more importantly, will give the delegated person a sense of direction which will lead them whenever they have to exercise discretion in the carrying out of your instructions.

Explain the purpose of the task

Don't just tell your team members what to do. First take the time to clearly explain the objectives and the overall purpose of the task that is being delegated.

Take the time to explain what outcome is needed and make your expectations crystal clear in this respect. Explain the desired results in ways that are specific and measurable. This will be easy to do if the task's objectives are clear in your own mind.

When explaining the task objectives, make sure that these are as specific as possible. You may leave room for discretion as to which steps should be taken to accomplish the task, but there should be no doubt or misunderstanding as to which objectives the task should achieve.

Tailor your explanation to the level of experience of the delegated person. Think about the person to whom you are talking, and make sure that you communicate in a manner and at a pace which is appropriate. Encourage the delegated person to seek clarification if necessary.

The importance of first explaining the objectives and the overall purpose of the delegated task, as opposed to the specific steps that need to be taken to complete the task, will be obvious if you consider the following example.

Imagine that you want to delegate to a member of your team the task of preparing and sending to your client regular updates on an ongoing case in which the client is involved. The purpose of the updates is, clearly, to keep the client regularly informed on the status of proceedings and appraised without delay of any development that might occur. You agree with your client that you will send them an update every Friday.

If you ask your assistant to prepare and send your client an update every Friday, your assistant will just do that and send your client an update every Friday even if a major development occurred on a Monday. Your assistant would not be at fault because they are simply following your instructions to the letter.

By contrast, if you ask your assistant to send your client an update every Friday but also explain to your assistant that the purpose of the reports is to keep the client regularly informed on the status of proceedings and appraised without delay of any development that might occur, chances are that if a major development occurs on a Monday, your assistant would come and ask you whether they should update your client immediately rather than wait until the end of the week.

Your assistant will be able to exercise judgment and react appropriately to changes and new information only if you have clearly explained to them what the objective and purpose of the delegated task are. Without this information, the delegated person will only be able to follow your instructions to the letter and will not be able to adapt to special circumstances as and when they arise.

Explain the steps

Only after you have clearly explained the objectives of the task that is being delegated, you can explain to the delegated person the specific steps that are required to achieve those objectives.

Assess the degree of direction required for the delegated person, based on their experience and level of confidence, and only give them the direction and help in planning their work that is strictly necessary in the circumstances.

You can divide the task into specific steps, suggest approaches and solutions, offer precedents, highlight important points and common mistakes but you should be careful not to micromanage the task and instead leave the delegated person room for discretion and opportunities to exercise their own judgment.

Unless you leave the delegated person scope to use their own thinking and judgment, that is room to decide how to get the task completed and its objectives achieved in full, the delegated person will not get a sense of ownership of the delegated task and will feel less motivated to perform it to a high standard.

If the delegated person does not feel that their skills and intellectual capabilities will be put at work in performing the task, they will think that the task at hand is dull, not stimulating enough, and accordingly they will feel demotivated.

When explaining how the task's objectives should be achieved, make sure that you avoid making decisions which the delegated person is capable of taking by themselves. The delegated person should take over the whole task and you should encourage them to do so.

Encourage the delegated person to complete the task in the manner they choose, but only as long as the results achieve the task's objectives. There may even be cases when you do not know how to complete the task yourself – in these cases, it will be critical to focus on the task's objectives as opposed to the specific steps required to achieve those objectives.

Once again, brief the delegated person in a manner and at a level and pace which is appropriate considering their experience and confidence level.

Check understanding

You should never presume that your instructions have been understood, especially when you are delegating to a junior assistant. Always ask the delegated person to summarize back to you their understanding of the instructions and the results that the delegated task should accomplish.

Test the delegated person's understanding frequently whilst talking to them and give them frequent opportunities to ask questions. It is sometimes the case that more junior members of staff are timid about admitting when something is unclear or think that they can work out the meaning of your instructions at a later stage, and perhaps ask someone else for assistance. Do not let this happen because it will probably cause misunderstanding and waste time at a later stage.
Check the delegated person's understanding until you feel comfortable that your instructions have been fully understood. It is your responsibility to check that the instructions you give are understood, and not vice versa.

Gain commitment

After having explained your instructions and ensured that they have been understood, you should gain the commitment of the delegated person to the task. Get buy-in from the delegated person that they are up to the task and willing to take responsibility for its successful completion.

It has been suggested that the more a delegated person has been encouraged to contribute to the planning of the specific steps and activities that are required to achieve the task's objectives, the more committed they will be to the task because they will get a sense of ownership in respect of delegated task. People are generally more excited about completing a task when they came up with the idea of how to do it, than if their supervisor tells them how to do it.

Try to take on board any suggestions the delegated person might have about how the task should be carried out. If you are able to create an atmosphere of collaboration and openness and induce the delegated person into thinking that they are being given a share in the success of the task and the whole project, you will be best placed to gain their full commitment to the task.

Similarly, you may find that having the delegated person actually pronounce words of commitment will increase their actual commitment to the task and clear in their mind any reservation they might have.

Agree a deadline

Always discuss your proposed deadline with the delegated person and ask them whether *they* think that your proposed deadline is realistic. Once again, the delegated person will feel more committed to a deadline upon which they feel they have been consulted.
Ask the delegated person to advise you immediately if, at any time during the performance of the task, they feel that it is not possible to meet the initial deadline.

Offer resources

Ask the delegated person what resources *they* think they need in order to complete the task well and within time. Ensure that those resources are made readily available.

Offer to provide support directly where needed and encourage the delegated person to seek your help when required. Provide access to any other members of your team who can help the delegated person complete the task, such as other colleagues, specialists and, where required, external advisers. As mentioned, every task you delegate should have enough complexity to stretch the delegated person, even if only a little. An element of support, therefore, should always be offered.

Offering support and resources will in effect ensure that the delegated person feels confident that they can complete the task. They will need to believe that they will be able to achieve the task which has been given to them if they are to succeed.

Make sure that the delegated person understands their individual responsibility and the limits of their authority, that is the extent to which they can rely on external resources. The delegated person should understand that being given the opportunity to seek help if required should not lessen their commitment to completing the project through their own work.

Agree on monitoring

Discuss with the delegated person what monitoring or measurement procedure *they* think should be put in place to monitor the progress of the delegated task. Monitoring procedures should keep you informed on the progress of the task whilst at the same time not give the delegated person the impression that you are constantly controlling them. Otherwise they might feel persecuted.

Agree on the frequency of feedback meetings or progress reports between you and the delegated person. Agreeing a reporting schedule in advance will also have a beneficial effect on the delegated person's motivation. Knowing that you are willing to monitor their progress as they go along will make the delegated person feel encouraged and not abandoned to the task.

6.   Monitoring Progress

After giving the delegated person appropriate instructions, you should start monitoring the progress of the task. You should not under any circumstances lose control of how the task is progressing nor assume that, unless you hear otherwise from the delegated person, everything is progressing as it should.

Remember that you are ultimately responsible for the delegated task and that the last thing you need is to receive an inadequate work product at the 11th hour. You should therefore remain vigilant and monitor the delegated person's performance on an ongoing basis.

You should in particular keep in touch with the delegated person and, without getting too close or being intrusive, check their progress. Be careful though not to put pressure on the delegated person otherwise your monitoring will have a negative effect on the delegated person's confidence and level of motivation. Make sure that your monitoring activities are in accordance with the reporting schedule you have agreed at the time of giving your instructions. Try to find the right balance between interest and interference.

Make also sure that, throughout the execution of the task, you maintain open lines of communication between you and the delegated person, working both ways.

Promptly inform the delegated person of any news, change in circumstances or change in instructions that might concern the execution of the task. Ideally the delegated person should have direct access to any relevant information. If this is not possible, it will be your responsibility to keep the delegated person fully and promptly informed.

Don't be afraid to give the delegated person open and direct access to the relevant information. The closer the delegated person is to the source of the information, the more involved they will feel and the level of their commitment will increase accordingly.

Maintaining open lines of communication also means that you should remain available at all times to respond to any question, concern or request for assistance the delegated person might have.

Be careful, however, not to get too involved in the execution of the delegated task and, above all, refuse making a decision on an issue unless the delegated person has identified all alternative solutions and, after having analysed the pros and cons of each solution, is able to provide a recommendation. You should always expect that all individuals reporting to you come to you giving you alternatives and suggestions when a problem exists rather than simply an explanation of the problem and a request for assistance.

Accordingly, whenever you are asked to make a decision on an issue concerning a task you have delegated, you should always ask the delegated person to think about all possible solutions before raising the matter with you. This is the only way for you to encourage a proactive attitude to problem-solving and independent thinking among your team members.

This approach will be extremely beneficial for the delegated person too. If you endorse their recommended solution, the delegated person will feel more confident and encouraged. If you disagree with their recommended solution, they will learn something new and feel more confident for having increased their knowledge and understanding.

When monitoring the delegated person's progress, check the actual work that is being produced rather then simply relying on the feedback you receive from the delegated person. For example, if you have asked the delegated person to draft an agreement, make sure that, when checking their progress, you actually take a look at the working draft of the agreement. You should always ask the delegated person to show you their work rather than merely asking whether everything is going well.

If the overall work is generally progressing well, refrain from giving unsolicited advice on how you think the work could be further improved and instead compliment the delegated person for the good progress made so far. You may want to leave your comments for a later stage, unless of course giving your suggestions at this stage would make a significant difference or would, for example, improve efficiency.

As a rule of thumb, whilst monitoring the progress of the delegated person, you should provide advice only when strictly necessary and not interfere without just cause. Be particularly careful not to allow perfectionism to kick in.

When you do give advice, make it clear whether you are offering a personal opinion or preference or professional advice and spend a few words praising the delegated person for their progress. This will give them encouragement and reinforce their confidence and commitment to the task.

If you notice that the delegated person is struggling with the delegated task and it looks as if they will not be able to complete it as they should for whatever reason, don't hesitate to get involved in the project directly or have another member of your team support the delegated person. Explain to the delegated person why you believe further assistance is required and make sure that, unless the delegated person has been negligent, they will not feel discouraged by their inability to deal with the delegated task on their own.

If you do get directly involved in the project or have another member of your team support the delegated person, ensure that the delegated person still perceives the task as their responsibility. Whatever the circumstances, try not to take the task from the delegated person and exclude them from further involvement. This would have a very detrimental impact on the delegated person and lessen their motivation and confidence.

7.   Providing Feedback

On receiving the final work from the delegated person, you will be responsible for checking the accuracy and level of quality of that work, and for providing the necessary feedback to the delegated person.

If you believe that the delegated person's work achieves its intended objectives and is fit for purposes, you may wish, depending on the circumstances, to accept the work in its entirety even if you feel that the work could be further improved by making a number of minor changes.

Only on very rare occasions the work you receive from the delegated person will be done as well as you would have done it, had you had the time to do it directly. You should never judge work done by others by what you expect you would do. Instead, limit yourself to assessing whether the work you receive achieves its intended objectives and is fit for purposes.

Don't be a perfectionist and be prepared to accept in its entirety work that is only "good enough" but meets in full the client's requirements, despite the fact that you would make minor changes to make it "perfect".

You may still want to show to the delegated person how the work could be improved but only for the sake of completeness and to make sure that your suggestions are incorporated the next time the delegated person is asked to produce similar work for you.

Accepting an acceptable piece of work in its entirety will have a very positive effect on the confidence of the delegated person and help improve their future performance and motivation. Getting the delegated person to continually redo acceptable work to make it perfect will, by contrast, demoralize and frustrate the delegated person and waste the time of both of you.

If you believe that the delegated person's work does not achieve its intended objectives, you should explain to them what changes you believe are required and ask them to make those changes until you receive work of a satisfactory quality.

Whatever the circumstances, resist the urge to make the required changes by yourself. This would be counter-productive for both of you because, unless taught otherwise, the delegated person will continue to make the same mistakes over and over again. There is also a risk that your team members will feel demoralised if you tell them that their work is inadequate and fix it yourself.

Having the delegated person fix their mistakes is generally the only way to make sure that those mistakes will not happen again.

When you provide feedback and comment upon the quality of the work the delegated person has done, you should try to be as specific, factual and accurate as possible. General observations and criticism will be of very little use to the delegated person and will only have a negative effect upon their morale.

Remember that the purpose of your feedback is to ensure that the delegated person understands exactly what mistakes they made and how their work could be improved, that is to say what procedures they could implement to prevent those mistakes from happening again.

Your feedback should be as fair and encouraging as possible. Deliver unfair feedback and you risk losing any goodwill you might have gained with the delegated person. Nobody wants to work for an unfair leader. If, by contrast, you can be fair and encouraging you will boost the delegated person's level of confidence, motivation and future commitment.

Remember also, when giving feedback, to deliver your comments in a manner and at a level and pace which is appropriate to the level of experience of the delegated person. Especially when dealing with junior members of your team, you should be very specific about how they have performed and any improvements that you believe are required.

Depending on the circumstances, you may wish to actively involve the delegated person in the evaluation of their own performance and encourage them to contribute to their own assessment. The delegated person might be more open to your comments if you make the evaluation phase of the delegation process a two-way process and seek input from them.

Ask the delegated person open ended questions about how they believe they have performed and, more importantly, encourage them to express any difficulties they might have encountered whilst carrying out the work. Encourage them to express any concern they might have had whilst carrying out the work and explain the approach taken to address those concerns.

If you wish to express any comment on the quality of the work delivered that might be perceived by the delegated person as being a criticism, use the so called "sandwich technique" whereby any negative comment is delivered in between two positive comments.

Point out something positive about the work first, then focus on the problem and after that express a final positive remark, be it a specific comment or a general word of praise and encouragement. This will have a very positive effect on the delegated person's confidence and motivation.

Always make a positive effort to identify aspects of the work delivered which could be praised, however bad you believe the work has been performed by the delegated person. Your aim should be to preserve the delegated person's confidence and motivation at all costs so that you can then gradually work on improving their skills.

Expressing negative comments without a word of praise and encouragement will only crush the delegated person's enthusiasm and motivation and be counter-productive for you. So recognise and praise the delegated person's effort and contributions however small these might have been.

As you probably know, people who receive regular recognition and praise at work are more engaged, productive and likely to stay with their firm longer. Therefore get into the habit of dispensing praise and acknowledgement as much as you can. Acknowledge good jobs, no matter how small, and recognise good performance and achievement on every occasion.

You may even want to express your words of praise publicly. Remember, by contrast, that a quiet word in private is usually the best way to give negative feedback.

Showing the final work to the delegated person will further contribute to their sense of accomplishment and motivation. Seeing the final product into which their work has been incorporated will contribute to the delegated person's sense of ownership and commitment to the whole project.

8.   Final Remarks: Errors and Failures

It is inevitable that from time to time errors and failures will occur in respect of work that has been delegated. Be prepared for these occurrences and try to put in place as many precautionary measures as possible. With appropriate measures in place, you should be able to catch mistakes before they become catastrophic.

Also be prepared, legally and emotionally, to take your fair share of responsibility for any failure that might occur. However badly the work might have been carried out by the delegated person, you are ultimately the person in charge of the delegation process, the person who delegated the task and should have monitored its progress closely.

In addition to taking full responsibility for the failure towards your clients, you should therefore take your share of responsibility for having failed to manage effectively the delegation process internally. Most of the time, in effect, failures and mistakes could have been avoided with better planning and monitoring from your side.

Be careful, however, not to be overly critical of yourself and make sure that you learn from your mistake. Take the time to identify and reflect upon the reasons for any failure and consider what systems and procedures you can implement in future in order to avoid the same mistake from happening again. Every mistake is a learning opportunity.

CHAPTER 8 – PUBLIC SPEAKING

1. Introduction

If you are like most lawyers, you will be required to speak in public quite a few times over your whole career. Whether to give an internal presentation to your colleagues or an external speech to existing or potential clients, there will be a number of occasions where you will be required to talk in front of a group of people, small or large, and even more if you are planning to use public speaking as a marketing tool.

When in front of an audience, it will be very important for you to be able to present your thoughts and ideas concisely and appear as someone who is competent, credible and comfortable speaking in public. Although most of the time you will not be expected to be a fabulous speaker, you will certainly be respected for getting your points across clearly and with validity.

If you are someone who enjoys the experience of speaking in public and find the experience pleasant and natural, the suggestions contained in this chapter will help you polish your existing skills as a speaker and become able to deliver even more slick presentations.

If, by contrast, you fear public speaking or simply find the experience uncomfortable most of the time, don't worry because you are not the only one. Anecdotal evidence suggests that the majority of lawyers have a difficult rapport with public speaking (especially if they are asked to speak in front of a large audience) and generally find the whole experience unnerving and awkward.

This chapter will help you overcome any fear you might have of speaking in public and give you the tools that you need to deliver, at any time, an excellent speech or presentation. By following the suggestions contained in the following pages, you will soon be able to stand in front of an audience with confidence and poise and become an even more skilled and confident lawyer.

2.   Preparing the Presentation

It is often said that a good speech begins before the speaker takes the stage to talk. An effective preparation is in effect key to a successful presentation. You should therefore spend as much time as you can preparing yourself for your speech.

Preliminary considerations

When preparing a presentation, the first thing you should consider is what specific purpose your presentation is intended to achieve. Before you even start to consider the contents of your presentation, take the time to consider whether the aim of your presentation will be to inform your audience, to describe or demonstrate something, to educate your audience, etc.

Are you trying to persuade your audience? Do you wish to discuss a problem which you or your firm is experiencing? Do you wish to illustrate a case or transaction on which you recently worked? Whatever your intentions, ensure that you clearly identify the purposes of your presentation so that you can work towards achieving those purposes by tailoring your presentation accordingly.

Take the time to then consider the audience to which your presentation will be delivered. Who will your audience be made up of? Other lawyers, existing clients, potential clients, or a combination of these? Ask yourself what your audience will already know about the topic you intend to address, why your audience should be interested in that topic and what is their attitude towards the topic.

Place yourself in your audience's shoes and ask yourself what would you want to hear if you were in the audience. Whatever your topic, you will have to tailor the contents of your presentation to your audience's needs if you wish them to find the contents interesting. Similarly, you will not be able to entertain or captivate your audience unless you know what your audience will find entertaining or captivating to start with.

Once you have addressed the above points, you should start researching your topic. Remember the ancient Latin maxim "rem tene, verba sequentur". The better you know your topic, the easier it is to talk about it.

There is generally no substitute for knowing your topic inside out so you will have to research your subject thoroughly if you do not already know that topic well. Only if you know your subject well, will you be able to exploit the subject's natural strengths and let your passion for the subject come through in your delivery.

Preparing the script

Once you have considered the above points, you can start preparing the script of your presentation.

Organise the material you have gathered in a logical progression, made up of an introduction (this should be a statement of your thesis in clear and succinct terms), a main body (a presentation of your main arguments, supported by accurate and up-to-date information) and a conclusion (a restatement of your thesis with a summary of the arguments presented).

Remember to keep things simple and short. Eliminate unnecessary details, and stick to the main points that your audience wants to hear. Whatever the make up of your audience, it is generally best to keep the main points of a speech to a minimum. You should never overwhelm your audience with too much information or details.

Ideally, you should be looking to make three or four main points, which you can then embellish with as many supporting arguments, success stories, anecdotes, quotes, and humour as you wish.

You might find it useful to divide the contents of your presentation into 'must know', 'should know' and 'could know', based on the characteristics of your audience. This will help you understand the main points on which you have to focus.

Bear in mind that the amount of time available to deliver your speech will invariably be limited. So try to keep things short and leave time for questions. It is generally better to leave your audience wanting to know more about your topic than having an audience who can't wait for your presentation to end. As a rule of thumb, you should aim to fill 75 per cent of the allotted time you are given to speak and leave the remaining 25 per cent for questions.

Think ahead about all the questions you might be asked and include a sketch question-and-answer section to your outline presentation. You do not want to be caught unprepared by a question that you could have anticipated nor appear to your audience as being unable to answer a question that they believe is fairly straightforward.

Once you are satisfied with the outline you have prepared, you should focus on the actual wording of your speech. Once again, bear in mind the make up of your audience. You should be looking to use everyday language as much as you can and avoid technical terms or keep them to a minimum whenever possible. Don't use pretentious language or words that are hard to pronounce.

Try to include in your script as many descriptive phrases as possible. These will have a powerful effect on your audience and help them to understand (and remember) your words and ideas. Also include as many stories, anecdotes, analogies and metaphors as possible. These will reinforce the key points of your presentation and have a lasting effect on your audience's memory.

Humour, in particular, will be an effective way to attract the audience's attention and drive a point home while at the same time amuse your audience. Use short jokes and personal anecdotes but make sure that your humorous material is appropriate for your audience.

Then write and rewrite the script until it sounds exactly right to your own ears.

Preparing all relevant material

As you are probably aware, the vast majority of presentations are nowadays prepared on PowerPoint so make sure that you know how to use that application at least at a very basic level. When reproducing your script on PowerPoint, try not to make excessive use of animation, sound clips or gaudy colours. These will only distract your audience from the contents of your presentation and may be inappropriate in certain circumstances.

Once the main script has been completed, consider whether you should prepare additional material for your own or your audience's use.

Consider whether preparing handouts to give to your audience would be beneficial. There are pros and cons. Handouts will give your audience something to take away with them and might work as a future reference and memory aid. They will, however, distract your audience during your speech and might even cause them to be less interested in your presentation knowing that a summary of your presentation will be available when required.

So far as your own needs are concerned, consider whether you should prepare any memory aids or notes to take with you on the day of the presentation. You might feel more confident knowing that you have some form of support material to which you can refer in case of need during your speech.

You might, for example, prepare an index card with keywords or key phrases or a set of 3″ x 5″ notecards with a summary of your main points. If you do so, use bullet points instead of sentences and make the text easy to read. Use a felt tip pen or bold large text characters and only use the top two-thirds of your cards to avoid having to look down.

As a general rule, this material should only assist you as a memory aid and not as a script from which to read your presentation. Reading from a script might give you confidence and ensure that nothing is forgotten or omitted but it will also make you look stiff and uninteresting and bore your audience.

Use your notes only occasionally, mainly to ensure that you are not skipping key points of your speech, but make sure that you remain able to speak directly to the audience for the most part of your presentation.

Rehearsing

Especially if you are nervous about having to give a presentation, you might be tempted to start rehearsing and practicing the delivery of your presentation too much. More often than not, rehearsing too much will have a detrimental effect on your delivery since it will deprive your presentation of any genuineness. How many times, for example, have you heard presentations that sound staged and contrived, in other words more like a monotonous recitation than a genuine speech?

Accordingly, be careful about practising and rehearsing too much. When preparing the delivery of your presentation, don't try to learn the whole presentation by heart. Instead, rehearse only until you feel comfortable about the presentation's contents and the relevant material and visual aids.

You want to sound as though you are having a conversation with your audience and not reciting something you have learnt by heart.

3.   The day of the presentation

What to dress

Make sure that the day of your speech you dress conservatively, in line with the dress code that your audience will follow and, very importantly, you do not wear any clothing or accessory that might distract your audience, for example, a fancy coloured tie, an unusual accessory or jewellery that glitters or jingles when you move or gesture. Similarly, make sure that your pockets are empty and do not contain anything that might make noise when you move.

As a speaker you want your audience to listen to what you are saying rather than to be interested in how you look.

Beating stage fright

Feeling some nervousness before giving a presentation will be natural and healthy and will happen even if you are an experienced public speaker.

If however you suffer from excessive nervousness, there are a number of suggestions that you can follow in order to remain calm on the day of your presentation and get rid of any stage fright you might experience on the day:

- Allow plenty of time to reach the place at which your presentation will be given. This will not only put you at ease, but it will give you an opportunity to socialize with your audience prior to your presentation and project that same friendly and confident attitude that will make your speech a success. Use any spare time prior to your presentation to also check the microphone and any visual aids you will use.

- Do some stretching exercises to get rid of any tension in your body muscles and open your jaw wide, relax and smile to get rid of any facial tension. Take very deep breathes just prior to the start of your speech. This will further relax your body, help your blood pressure to lower and your mind to clear. You may want to follow the suggestions given in the Stress Management chapter on this book.

- Sit quietly for a few minutes before your speech to gather your thoughts. Clear your mind by visualising a pleasant and calming scene. Then, once you are relaxed, run quickly through your slides and notes to regain a sense of familiarity from that material. This should reassure you that everything is under control.

- Use visualization techniques. Close your eyes and visualize yourself delivering your presentation with poise and confidence.

Imagine yourself speaking, your voice loud, clear, and assured. Visualise yourself receiving positive feedback from your audience. When you visualize yourself as successful, you will be successful.

- Don't apologize. You should never mention your nervousness at the start of your speech or apologize for any problems you think you will have with your speech. You may be calling the audience's attention to something they would not otherwise have noticed.

Practise all of the above suggestions to find the ones that work best for you. Stage fright will soon become only a reminiscence of the past.

4.   Delivering Your Presentation: Body Language

The importance of body language has already been highlighted in a previous chapter of this book. Non-verbal communication, which is mainly comprised of body language and voice tone, plays a more important role than verbal communication most of the time.

This is particularly true in relation to public speaking. It has been suggested that on average an audience determines whether or not a speaker is credible within seven seconds of the speaker getting on stage and that an audience's judgment is based not on what the speaker says but on the speaker's body language and voice tone.

When you are giving a presentation you should therefore make sure that both your voice tone and body language transmit a message of confidence, poise and professionalism. Being able to monitor and manage your voice tone and body language effectively will be, most of the time, key to a successful presentation.

General posture

Your general posture should be that of a relaxed and confident speaker. In principle, and subject to the suggestions below, you should try to be as genuine and natural as you are when you speak to your family and friends.

If you are standing at a lectern, make sure that you adopt an open and relaxed posture and keep you feet grounded to the floor. Stand up straight and keep your body centred. You do this by keeping your feet directly under your hips. This is the most stable position for public speaking. Under no circumstances should you lean on the lectern.

If your whole body is on view, you must establish a whole-body approach from the start of your presentation. You should try to project a strong image. Standing straight on both feet will be particularly important in these circumstances. Keep the front of the body fully exposed to the audience even when you are pointing at a flip chart.

When you stand on the stage, monitor your body to make sure that you are not shifting weight from one foot to the other or rocking forwards and backwards on the spot. These movements can be very distracting and annoying for the audience and, once started, they may be hard to stop. So just don't start them.

Facial Expression

Your facial expression will be key if you wish to retain the audience's attention and persuade them about the validity of your ideas and messages. Your audience will watch your face during your presentation and seek a confirmation from your face about the validity of your verbal message.

Make sure that you do not frown and that your face projects sincerity, conviction, and credibility. Put a warm smile on your face before you begin to speak and keep it throughout your presentation. This will warm up your audience quickly, put them at ease and make the whole experience of listening to your presentation a pleasurable one.

Be careful, however, not adopt any facial expression that does not really belong to you. Don't try to copy the facial expression or style of someone else. Just because a colleague of yours usually starts his or her presentations by telling a story with an exaggerated facial expressions does not mean that the same style will work for you.

Find your own style and stick to it. Whatever you do, don't overdo it otherwise you will appear unnatural and stiff.

Eye contact

Eye contact has been described as the cement that binds together the speaker and their audience. Whether you are addressing a small or large audience, you should make eye contact with your audience because that will involve them in your presentation and keep them interested.

By looking at each member of your audience individually will be able to convince them that you are interested in them and that you care about their reactions to what you are saying. Making eye contact will give each listener the impression that you are talking directly to him or her.

Make eye contact with each member of your audience in turn for about three seconds and every now and then glance at the whole audience. Do the same even if you are addressing a large audience in which case, since it will be impossible to make eye contact with everyone, you should pick out one or two individuals in each section of your audience and make eye contact with them in turn.

Making eye contact with your audience will also be a very effective way to check your audience's attentiveness and concentration. By looking at your audience, you will gain a feeling of how your audience is reacting to your presentation. Gauge your audience's reactions and adjust your presentation accordingly.

If, for example, you notice that most of the audience is not looking at you, chances are that they are not listening either. Do not feel discouraged in this case. Rather, find a way to regain your audience's attention before it is too late. Try, for example, to alter your voice tone, make a short pause or introduce some humour. Keep trying until you succeed in regaining their attention (or you run out of time).

If, by contrast, you notice that the majority of the audience returns your eye contact, nods at you or generally look interested, keep doing what you are doing and be confident that your presentation will be a success.

Body movements

When delivering a presentation, you should never make any body movements without a reason. The eye is inevitably attracted to a moving object, so any body movement you make during your speech will attract the attention of your audience. Move too much or at inappropriate times and you will have lost the attention of your audience. If you are going to move, therefore, make sure that you move with intention.

If you learn to move your body in a controlled and purposeful manner, you will become able to use your body movements as an additional communication tool to reinforce the contents of your verbal communication, attract your audience's attention and burn any nervous energy you might have accumulated in your body.

Remember the following three types of body movement: 1) step forward if you are arriving at an important point; 2) step backward if you have concluded an idea and want the audience to relax for a moment; 3) move laterally if you wish to leave a topic or idea and take up a new one.

Practise the above body movements until you feel confident enough to make use of them during your presentations. Mastering those movements will be a very powerful communicating tool.

Gesturing

As with body movements, you should never make any gesture or take any action that is unrelated to the contents of your speech. Any gesture or action will draw your audience's attention so you should be careful not to engage in any unrelated mannerisms.

Unrelated mannerism includes gestures like gripping or leaning on the lectern, tapping your fingers, frowning, fidgeting with cufflinks, buttons or jewellery, and so on. Most of the time these gestures will be the physical manifestation of your nervousness, something that you should keep under control.

Regrettably, it is often the case that the above gestures are performed unconsciously by a speaker so you might not be able to notice what you are doing while you are doing it. If you suspect that this is your case, the only way to identify what kind of mannerism affects you is to ask a friend who is part of your audience or, if you are brave enough, to videotape yourself giving the presentation. Once you have identified any distracting mannerism that may affect you, you will be able to keep it under control during your next presentation.

Ensure that all your gestures are natural and suit your words and the message you wish to deliver. Your gestures should be lively and distinct if they are to convey the intended impression. Do not hesitate nor inhibit a movement once started.

Make sure that your gestures are vigorous enough to be convincing yet smooth enough and broad enough to be clearly visible without being overpowering. This will be particularly important if you are delivering your presentation to a large audience. Amplify your movements slightly if you wish your gestures to be effective.

Voice tone

In principle, you should try to deliver your presentation using a natural tone, the same conversational tone that you would use in a normal conversation. This applies whether you are using a microphone or not.

Be particularly careful for any sign of nervousness in your voice. An unnaturally high or low voice pitch, or speaking too fast, will immediately be perceived by your audience as a sign of nervousness. If this happens, simply relax, make a deep breath and gain back control over your voice.

Make sure that you speak a little louder than you would otherwise. Speak loud enough so that your entire audience, and not just the first few rows, can hear you. Do not yell, however, even if you find that this would be the only way to reach the whole of your audience.

Try to direct your voice to your audience. Imagine that when you speak a laser beam travels from your mouth to your audience and that you are in control of where that laser beam is directed. Move it across your audience so as to reach everyone in turn.

Also be aware of the speed at which you speak. When delivering a presentation you should speak at a slighter slower pace than you would otherwise, so that you can pronounce words clearly and give your audience to reflect on what you are saying as you go along.

5. Delivering Your Presentation: Practical Suggestions

The following suggestions will further assist you during your presentation.

Remember to gain attention

When your presentation first starts, do not commence straight away talking about your topic. Instead, start with an opener to gain the attention of your audience. Often, the note on which you start will carry on all the way through your presentation.

You could, for example, tease your audience, tell an appropriate joke or ask your audience a question. Whatever you choose to do, remember not to commence your real presentation until you have captured your audience's attention.

Add humour

Proper humour is always appropriate. So add as much humour to your presentation as you can. Just make sure that your humour is appropriate to the circumstances and your audience.

Deliver with passion

You probably already know how catchy enthusiasm can be. So be passionate about your topic when you deliver your presentation. Speak with conviction and believe in what you are saying. Your audience will be immediately captured by your enthusiasm.

Keep going

If you are momentarily lost or if you notice you made an error or skipped an important part of your presentation, correct your error or omission with the same confidence you have used until that moment and keep going.

Do not attract the audience's attention to your error or omission. Chances are that your audience has not even noticed it. So do not make excuses or apologise. Just keep going with confidence.

Prepare to be flexible

Be flexible and prepared for the unexpected. Monitor your audience and, if you notice that things are not progressing the way you would like them to progress, adjust and adapt.

If what you have prepared is not getting across to your audience, change your strategy immediately and keep trying different things until you get your desired outcome. Likewise, if you notice you are running short of time, know what you can safely drop and, if you have extra time, know what can effectively add. Plan to be flexible.

Know your conclusion

Do not let you presentation or speech drag on endlessly. Once you have presented the main points of your speech and covered your main objectives, conclude your speech. Your audience will appreciate your efforts to be succinct. It is generally better to leave your audience wanting to know more about your topic than having an audience who can't wait for your presentation to end.

Summarise your main points when concluding your presentation and leave your audience with a positive impression and a sense of completion.

Be appreciative

At the end of your presentation, remember to thank your audience and the person or persons who asked you to give the speech.

CHAPTER 9 - TIME AND STRESS MANAGEMENT

1.   Introduction

Effective time management skills, the ability to keep stress under control and the ability to work efficiency will be crucial to you if you wish to succeed as a lawyer.

Good time management and stress management skills are a pre-condition to success within the legal profession. As you probably know, it doesn't really matter how much time you spend in the office. What matters is what you accomplish whilst there and how many chargeable hours you bill during your day.

A lawyer who lacks time management skills and is unable to perform consistently at a high level will struggle to achieve results and profitability for their practice despite the fact that they might be permanently busy.

Likewise, a lawyer who is unable to keep their stress levels under control and use stress to improve upon their performance effectiveness will eventually burn out and suffer exhaustion.

If you wish to become a successful lawyer you will therefore have to learn how to manage your time effectively, keep your stress levels under control and improve upon your productivity and effectiveness.

You will have to learn how to make the most of every minute of your life, whether spent in the office doing work or outside the office dealing with any other aspect of your life (family, friends, etc.), and how to maintain your stress at an optimal level so that your stress can give you energy, ambition, and enthusiasm without causing distress or harming your health and general wellbeing.

The suggestions contained in this chapter will help you to achieve these goals. They will show you how you can increase your level of efficiency by allocating your time more effectively and keeping your stress levels under control.

2. Time Management: Review Your Current Situation

To begin managing your time more effectively you first need to gain a clear picture of how you currently use your time. The most effective way to do this is by writing a diary for one week as to how you spend your days.

Write down all the activities you carry out during your day and the time you spend on each of them. Track, for example, how much time you spend sleeping each night, how much time you spend having breakfast, how much time you spend grooming, how much time you spend commuting to and from work every day, how much time you spend in the office and so on.

Take a note of how you actually make use of your time whilst in the office and track, for example, how much time you spend talking to your colleagues, surfing the internet and dealing with paperwork or other chores as opposed to how much time you actually spend doing billable work.

At the end of the week, find a relaxed moment to examine your diary. You will probably be surprised to see on paper how your time all adds up together. Take a moment to analyse the data in front of you, discover patterns that you have not noticed before and, above all, identify the activities that frankly represent a waste of your time. These will typically be all those activities that do not provide any obvious benefit to your life but still take up some of your time.

If, whilst carrying out this review, you feel that your daily schedule does not make you accomplish all that you wish to accomplish during your day, the time has come for you to start managing your time more efficiently.

3. Prioritise

The first step you should take towards achieving a more efficient use of your time is to understand that, since time is a limited resource, you are not generally in a position to achieve everything you would like to achieve.

Learn to prioritise things and take a moment to carefully consider what is important to you so far as your work and, more generally, your life are concerned.

Take the time to consider every category of your life including health, finance, career, family, etc. and establish, clear objectives for each category. Then rank the categories in order of importance.

Ask yourself, for example, whether, if you were to choose, you would put your job before your family, dining out with a friend before your health, going to the latest movie above exercising in the gym, enjoying a high-consumption lifestyle above saving for a secure retirement, and so on.

Once you have established your priorities, you can ask yourself whether your current allocation of time is fully congruent with your priorities. Since you do not have the time and energy to do all the things that in principle you would like to do, you must give priority to certain things over others. Ask yourself whether at the moment you are really prioritising your activities according to how important they are to you.

Examine how you have been spending your time during the week you were tracking your activities and honestly consider whether you really used all your time resources to pursue what is most important to you.

Say, for example, you believe that you have reached a stage in your career when it would be more important for you to focus on business development activities rather than fee-earning activities. Did you devote during that week sufficient time to business development activities as opposed to fee-earning activities?

If you find that a discrepancy or lack of alignment exists between the way you spend your time and your priorities, you should reallocate your time in a way that is more consistent with your priorities.

Identify which activities you could let go of in order to free up time to dedicate to the pursuit of your most important goals. Identify which habits you could change in order to become more efficient when pursuing those goals. Identify ways to ease up on things that are not really important and reorganize your activities to eliminate waste and maximize every minute of your time.

You will then be able to start introducing any necessary change into your daily routine and work habits. Once again, focus your energies on the pursuit of what is most important to you and don't be afraid to discontinue activities that are not really instrumental to achieving your personal and professional goals. If an activity that is part of your daily routine does nothing to further your most important objectives, why should you continue to do it?

Learn to say no to things that don't fit into what you really want out of your life and work. As mentioned, if you wish to accomplish more of the things that are important to you, you have to dedicate yourself to the pursuit of those things full-time and abandon any other thing that can distract you from your goals.

By following this time management technique, you will create more space to do and have more of the things in life that are really meaningful to you. By embracing your goals and objectives in full and focusing all your energies on those objectives, you will become much more efficient and will be on the right path to accomplish more.

4.   The Mayonnaise Jar

The importance of prioritizing the things that are most important at the expense of any other thing is the subject of a beautiful story, known as "the mayonnaise jar and the coffee story", which is reproduced below.

"A professor stands before his philosophy class and has some items in front of him. When the class begins, wordlessly, he picks up a very large and empty mayonnaise jar and proceeds to fill it with golf balls. He then asks the students if the jar is full. They agree that it was.

The professor then picks up a box of pebbles and pours them into the jar. He shakes the jar lightly. The pebbles roll into the open areas between the golf balls. He then asks the students again if the jar is full. They agree it was.

The professor next picks up a box of sand and pours it into the jar. Of course, the sand fills up everything else. He asks once more if the jar is full. The students respond with a "yes."

The professor then produces two cups of coffee from under the table and pours the entire contents into the jar, effectively filling the empty space between the sand. The students laugh.

"Now," says the professor, as the laughter subsided, "I want you to recognize that this jar represents your life. The golf balls are the important things. Your family, your children, your faith, your health, your friends, and your favourite passions. Things that if everything else was lost and only they remained, your life would still be full. The pebbles are the other things that matter. Your career, your house, and your car. The sand is everything else. The small stuff."

"If you put the sand into the jar first," he continues, "there is no room for the pebbles or the golf balls. The same goes for life. If you spend all your time and energy on the small stuff, you will never have room for the things that are important to you. Pay attention to the things that are critical to your happiness. Play with your children. Take time to get medical checkups. Take your partner out to dinner. There will always be time to clean the house and fix something. Take care of the golf balls first, the things that really matter. Set your priorities. The rest is just sand."

One of the students raises her hand and inquires what the coffee represented. The professor smiles. "I'm glad you asked. It just goes to show you that no matter how full your life may seem, there's always room for a couple of cups of coffee with a friend."

Manage your time based on your real priorities and you will be on the right way to a life of happiness and achievement.

5.   Time Planning and "To Do" Lists

Once you have set your priorities, you can start planning how to achieve your goals and schedule all your required tasks and activities. Prepare annual and monthly "to do" lists where you can list the activities that you wish to carry out in order to accomplish your goals and write down when you are planning to carry out those activities.

Try to be as specific as possible so far as the timing of those activities is concerned. The more precise you are, the more focused you will be when the time comes to work out your schedule. Having clear deadlines will prevent procrastination on your part. If it helps, you might even want to turn the to do's into time specific appointments.

Keep your annual and monthly lists as an important point of reference for the preparation of your shorter-term "to do" lists, which are weekly and daily lists that you will prepare at the end of each day for the following day and at the end of each week for the following week.

The main purpose of your annual, monthly and weekly "to do" lists will be to keep you focused on your long-term goals and priorities. The main purpose of your daily lists will be to increase your daily effectiveness and productivity.

Always prepare your daily list a day in advance. This way you will know, every day, the most important tasks that you have to accomplish that day before hitting your desk in the morning. Having planned your day a day in advance will substantially increase your effectiveness.

Include in your daily list all the tasks that you wish to complete the following day and rank each task in accordance with its importance and urgency. Identify in particular the top three most important tasks that *must* be completed whatever happens that day. Number them 1, 2 and 3 in order of importance and commit yourself to completing those tasks whatever happens.

Then select, in order of importance, the second three most important tasks and number them 4, 5, and 6. Commit yourself, however, not to spend time on those tasks until the top three most important tasks have been completed.

You could add further items to your daily list if you wish to. Be realistic, however, about how many tasks you can really complete in one day. It is generally a good sign if you are willing to go the extra mile but don't overstretch yourself if you don't have to.

If you were to accomplish five or six items on your "to do" list each day, you could still consider it a very productive day. Five or six tasks a day adds up to 25 to 30 tasks completed in a week.

When the day begins, work out each item on your list in order of priority and remain focused. Do first things first and, when you start a task, forget about all other items on your list and concentrate exclusively on the task at hand. Do not be distracted by the other items on your list. You will get to them later. If necessary, clear your desk of all the papers that are unrelated to the task at hand. This is a very important time management tool.

Once you have finished a task, move on to the next one until you have been through all the tasks on your list, at which point in time you will feel a great sense of accomplishment and satisfaction.

Whatever your objectives and priorities are, planning and prioritizing your activities on a daily, weekly and monthly basis will increase your chances of accomplishing your goals within your timescale, dramatically improving your level of efficiency and helping you become a much more productive person.

7.   Time Management: Practical Suggestions

The following practical suggestions will help you to further improve your effectiveness and make the most of your time.

Learn to say "No"

Learning to say no when appropriate will be key if you wish to remain focused on the most important tasks you set yourself to complete during a day.

Practise saying "No" whenever you are asked to deal with something you genuinely do not have time for or that you believe is less important than the task you are currently dealing with, although it may seem "urgent".
Don't let other people distract you from your schedule of important tasks since any unplanned digression will result in a waste of time and loss of concentration. Be careful, in particular, not get embroiled in the so called "crisis management" activities that almost invariably only result in a trail of unfinished projects, unreturned phone calls and unread e-mails.

Don't over-commit yourself by taking on more than you can possibly accomplish. Likewise, don't let people take it for granted that you are there to assist them even when you objectively do not have time for them.

Learn the difference between urgent and important and politely, but firmly, say "No" to any urgent but unimportant unplanned task you are asked to deal with during your day.

Under-promise and over-deliver

You may have heard this before. Especially when dealing with clients, resist the temptation to agree deadlines that might be too tight and that you might not be able to meet if problems arise.

Instead, agree a deadline that you can comfortably meet and, where the circumstances so permit, deliver the promised work in advance of your deadline.

For example, if you can send out a draft contract by Tuesday noon, tell your client they will receive it by Wednesday afternoon. Then let them have the work on Tuesday if you can.

Don't be a perfectionist

Resist the temptation to seek perfection and settle instead for producing work that is "only" of high quality. Trying to be perfect most of the time will only reduce your level of efficiency, without bringing any material benefit to you or your clients.

Adding that additional clause to a contract that is already very comprehensive, spending time to perfect the wording of a document that is already accurately drafted, amending a document produced by someone else for the sake of having it done the way you like it and any other similar perfection-seeking behaviour will only result in a waste of your time.

When you find yourself adding your final touches to a document, ask yourself whether you are actually making valuable use of your time. If the answer is no, stop immediately and devote yourself to other more productive undertakings.

Relinquish any anxious need you might have to be and be seen as perfect by your clients and colleagues and be instead prepared to "settle" for being a good (but more efficient) lawyer.

Delegate work

The importance of delegating as many task as you possibly can to your team members has been discussed in a previous chapter of this book.

It is worth emphasising again that making effective use of delegation is an essential tool if you wish to achieve a higher level of productivity whilst reducing your workload at the same time. When you are presented with any task, ask yourself whether it would make more sense delegating that task to a member of your team and, if the answer is yes, proceed accordingly.

Handle paper once only

When you are dealing with paperwork, decide immediately whether you should respond, refer, file or destroy the relevant paperwork. Deal with paper rather than shuffling it around your desk with the intention to deal with it at a later time.

When you read an e-mail or a letter, process it right then. Decide on the spot what needs to be done with that communication and act immediately. If you fail to do this, you will have to go through the exact same decision process the next time that you examine that e-mail or letter.

Control interruptions

When you are focusing on a task, take precautionary measures to prevent any unwanted interruption.

Measures could include, for example, turning your telephone to voicemail, ignoring any incoming e-mails and informing your secretary that you do not wish to be disturbed by anyone. If someone approaches you, politely explain that you are concentrating on a very important task and ask them if you could get back to them at a later time.

Depending on how busy you are during a day, you might even decide to answer your phone, voice mail and check e-mail only at specific intervals and not as and when communications arrive. As you probably already know, nothing can break concentration more than having a client call you about a matter unrelated to what you are currently working on.

Research suggests that interruptions typically make a worker lose between one and two hours a day. Bear this in mind when you are planning your day and don't be afraid to take any precautionary measures that are required to safeguard your time and effectiveness.

Keep your desk uncluttered

Keeping your desk uncluttered and maintaining an efficient documentation retrieval system will help you maintain a high level of concentration and effectiveness.

It has been suggested that working in front of a clear and well-organized desk helps the mind to think clearly and maintain concentration.

Meetings

Research suggests that about a third of the time spent in meetings is wasted for a number of reasons, including poor meeting management and lack of planning. You should therefore keep the amount of time you spend in meetings under control and skip meetings or send someone else where appropriate.

However remember that, as mentioned in a previous chapter, meetings are important to build relationships with the people you work with, your colleagues and clients.

Review Your Routine

Keep your daily routine under constant review to see whether it needs some adjusting. Regularly ask yourself whether any action you take as part of your daily routine contributes to your effectiveness and, if not, discontinue it or improve upon it. Only retain habits and routines that positively contribute to your efficiency and wellbeing.

Consider, for example, the habit of staying up late at night in front of the TV as opposed to the habit of frequenting a gym, or the habit of tidying up your desk and files every once in a while as opposed to taking 5 minutes every day to keep things always in order.

A minor improvement in your daily routine, however trivial or insignificant it might seem, will have a huge consequence on your productivity in the long term.

If you keep your daily routines under constant review you will achieve a higher level of effectiveness.

8.   Stress Management: Identify your Stress factors

In order to take control of your stress levels you first need to gain a clear understanding of the factors, thoughts, activities and worries that most stress you on a day-to-day basis. You will not be able to fight your stress unless you precisely identify what stresses you, that is your stress factors.

Using an exercise similar to the exercise described earlier in this section, for a whole week, keep a diary where you write down how stressed you feel every hour of your day.

Take a note of how stressed you feel when you wake up in the morning, when you are travelling to work, when you are in the office, during your lunch break and so on until the time you go to bed at night. Give a value from 1 to 5 to the level of your perceived stress, where 1 is very low and 5 is very high.

Monitor both your emotional and physical reactions to every stressful situation that occurs and write down, for example, whether you feel anxious, nervous, directionless, confused or unproductive or, so far as your physical reactions are concerned, tense, still or otherwise physically disturbed.

Take a note of the sources of your stress. Try to identify what causes you to feel dissatisfied, irritable or frustrated when you experience those feelings.

Be careful not to underestimate the level of stress that an apparently trivial factor might cause. You may already know how much stress can be caused by an apparently small thing such as an incorrectly positioned chair or computer screen or a continuous noise.

Therefore, however trivial a stressful factor might be, don't ignore it and instead add it to your list. In fact, the more you argue in your mind about the insignificance of a stressful factor, the more likely it is that that factor is a cause of considerable stress.

At the end of the week, find a relaxed moment to examine your diary. Try to look for repeating patterns and trends in the way your stress evolves during your day and identify the activities and situations that are typically the source of high stress levels. Then summarize your findings and list all the major external and internal stressors that affect your daily life.

Ask yourself whether each of the stressful factors you have identified really constitutes something you should worry about. Writing usually provides perspective on situations. Having all your stressful factors in front of you might make you realize that sometimes you worry about things that should not really worry you.

Experience, for example, might have showed you that you should not really worry about some of the things you were worrying about at the early stage of your career, for example, the happening of events that have never materialised. Have all these years shown you that you should not really worry about those things? If so, let go of all those imaginary concerns and worries and make a commitment not to get stressed about them ever again.

Next focus your attention on all the remaining items on your list and consider whether, rather than keep worrying about those things, you could take a proactive action to tackle them.

Action could be taken or systems put in place which would minimize the chance of your worries materializing, eliminate or reduce your exposure to those things or reduce the intensity of the relevant stress factors.

Whatever stresses you, feeling like a victim will only increase your feelings of helplessness and anguish. Therefore avoid feeling like a victim and instead make a positive effort to find a solution to your problems. Identifying a solution to a problem is easier if your mind is clear from stress and worries.

Some researchers believe that every stress factor is simply an internal, mental, psychological process which has no existence in the physical world and only exists in the human mind. It can accordingly be eliminated altogether if the person who suffers from it takes the time to think about it and elaborate upon it.

Whether this is true or not, you will certainly benefit immensely if you take the time, sooner rather than later, to reflect upon what worries and stresses you most especially if, after having identified the causes of your worries and stress, you take an active step to change your situation (where possible).

Remember the Serenity Prayer: "God grant me the courage to change the things I can change; the serenity to accept the things I cannot change; and the wisdom to know the difference."

8.   The Importance of a Balanced Lifestyle

It may sound like a cliché, but it is true that you will enjoy a higher level of energy and resilience to stress if you live a healthy and balanced lifestyle. A healthy and balanced lifestyle will help you restore your energies when you feel depleted, sustain your effectiveness when you feel overwhelmed and ensure that you do not suffer from physical or psychological burnout.

A healthy lifestyle means, as you probably know, getting enough sleep, exercising regularly, maintaining a well-balanced and nutritious diet and avoiding nicotine, excessive caffeine, alcohol and other stimulants.

A healthy lifestyle also means devoting yourself regularly to pleasurable and relaxing activities, every day, even if it is only for 10 minutes. Pleasurable and relaxing activities might be listening to your favourite music, talking to a friend about your problems, getting a massage, taking a hot bath, reading a book or watching TV with your family. Or they might simply be taking the time in the morning to be silent, gaze out the window, meditate or enjoy other peaceful moments.

Take the time to identify what activities you find more enjoyable and relaxing and make sure that all these activities are included in your daily schedule under the heading "recreational activities" or "peaceful moments".

Do not make the mistake of thinking that you can live without these activities and can instead devote all your time and energy to your work. Although these activities might appear unproductive and sometimes just a waste of time, they play an essential role in refilling your energy levels. Without them, you are bound to run out of energy sooner or later.

Learn to cherish these activities and peaceful moments and prioritise them over your work where necessary. Make sure that, whatever your circumstances and however busy you might be, you always find the time for them. Learn to pay yourself first.

9.   Relaxation Techniques

In order to keep your stress levels under control, you should recognize your stress symptoms as they build up during the day and take action against them immediately, so as to prevent the building-up of negativity and anxiety before it becomes too late. Don't let tension and stress build up.

Whilst every person has their own unique stress signals, the three most common indicators of stress are shallow breathing, muscle tension and increased heart rate. You should therefore pay particular attention to your breathing, muscle tension and heart rate as you progress your day.

Be on the lookout, for example, for any sign of muscle tension that may appear as you travel to work in the morning, and keep you breathing and heart beat under control whilst sitting at your desk during the day. If you notice that your body is building up tension, that means that your stress levels are starting to increase.

If you find any symptom of stress in your body, stop for a few moments and collect yourself. Step away from what is stressing you and take a few deep breaths. Slow, deep breathing will bring your heart rate and respiration back to normal.

Breathing from your diaphragm, in particular, will oxygenate your blood and help you relax almost instantly. If you are new to diaphragm breathing, the way you do it is simple. Put your hand on your abdomen just below the navel and inhale slowly through your nose pushing down the air into your body as much as you can. If you are doing this correctly, your hand should move out as your belly expands. Hold the breath for a few seconds, then exhale slowly.

Repeat this exercise three or four times until you feel that any excessive tension has been released from your body. Then take a moment to notice the difference in what it feels like to be tense and then to be relaxed again.

If however you find that taking a few deep breaths did not release all the tension you accumulated in your body, it is probably time to combine deep breathing with other more specific relaxation techniques.

The following are the most common:

- Stand up and stretch. Doing a quick exercise will help you release muscle tension and breath with your diaphragm. Stretch your arms out from your sides and shake your hands vigorously for about 10 seconds. Then do the same with your legs and feet. Shaking it up will help you release muscle tension.

- Stand up and smile. Smiling is a two-way mechanism. People smile when they are relaxed and happy, but smiling when you do not feel like smiling can somehow force you to feel happy again. This is because smiling transmits nerve impulses from the facial muscles to the limbic system, a key emotional centre in the brain, tilting the neurochemical balance towards happiness again. Go ahead and try it.

- Take a short walk. Taking a short walk will force you to breathe more deeply and improve blood circulation. It will also relax your muscles.

- Put things into context. Using a scale of 1 to 10, with 1 being the equivalent of a minor hassle and 10 being a true catastrophe, assign a number to whatever it is that is making you feel anxious. This will provide perspective and help you put the situation you are facing into context. You may find that most of the problems you are facing can be given a value of 3 to 5 and, as such, are not as disastrous as you initially thought they were.

- Visualize calm. It may sound New Age, but many people find that visualizing calm is a highly effective way of reducing accumulated stress. Close your eyes, take three long, slow breaths, and spend a couple of minutes picturing a relaxing scene. Imagine that you are in a hot bath and a warm wave of relaxation permeates your body. Focus on the details (the sensations, the sights, the sounds, the smells) and enjoy those moments. If you do not remember what a hot bath feels like, maybe it is time to try it again!

- Straighten Up. It has been suggested that slouching on a chair and generally maintaining an incorrect body posture may contribute to accumulating stress. This is because slouching restricts breathing and reduces blood and oxygen flow to the brain. If you find yourself slouching on your chair or otherwise sitting improperly, try to straighten up. This will promote circulation, increase oxygen levels in your blood and help lessen muscle tension, all of which is likely to make you feel more relaxed.

Try all of the above techniques and find the ones that work best for you. Then use them every time you are facing a stressful situation. Being able to manage your stress effectively will be an invaluable tool to use both in your work and personal life.

BIBLIOGRAPHY AND FURTHER READING

It is not possible to provide a complete list of the many authors who have researched and written on the topics covered by this book. Listed below are the authors on whose books, articles and publications this book is mostly based. Readers are encouraged to read directly the relevant publications if they wish to further their knowledge of the relevant topics.

Non-Verbal Communication

On communication in general and emotional intelligence:
* Introducing NLP Neuro-Linguistic Programming by Joseph O'Connor and John Seymour (HarperCollins 2003)
* Mastering Communication by Nicki Stanton (Palgrave Macmillan 2004)
* Emotional Intelligence by Daniel P. Goleman (Bantam Books 2005)
* Working with Emotional Intelligence by Daniel Goleman (Bloomsbury Publishing 1999)
* Emotional Intelligence: Why It Can Matter More Than IQ by Daniel Goleman (Bloomsbury Publishing PL 1996)

On dressing finesse:
* Secrets of Style: "Instyle's" Complete Guide to Dressing Your Best Every Day by Lisa Arbetter (Warner Books 2003)
* A Guide to Elegance: A Complete Guide for the Woman Who Wants to Be Well and Properly Dressed for Every Occasion by Genevieve Antoine Dariaux (HarperCollins Publishers 2003)
* Dressing the Man by Alan Flusser (HarperCollins 2003)
* A Well-dressed Gentleman's Pocket Guide by Oscar Lenius (Prion Books 1998)

On non-verbal communication in general and body language:
* The Definitive Book of Body Language: How to Read Others' Attitudes by Their Gestures by Allan Pease and Barbara Pease (Orion 2005)
* Peoplewatching: The Desmond Morris Guide to Body Language by Desmond Morris (Vintage 2002)
* Body Language at Work: Read Signs and Make the Right Moves by Peter Clayton (Hamlyn 2003)

- Visible Thought: The New Psychology of Body Language by Geoffrey Beattie (Routledge 2003)
- Body Language by David Lambert and Diagram Group (Collins 2004)
- Body Language: Make the Most of Your Professional and Personal Life by Learning to Read and Use the Body's Secret Signals by Susan Quilliam (Carlton Books 2004)
- The Power of Handshaking: For Peak Performance Worldwide (Capital Ideas for Business & Personal Development) by Dorothea Johnson and Robert Brown (Capital Books 2004)

Specifically on voice tone:
- Set Your Voice Free: How to Get the Singing or Speaking Voice You Want by R. Love (Little, Brown & Company 2003)

Verbal Communication

On verbal communication:
- Language and Creativity: The Art of Common Talk by Ronald Carter (Routledge 2004)
- Crucial Conversations: Tools for Talking When Stakes Are High by Kerry Patterson, Joseph Grenny, Ron McMillan, Al Switzler (McGraw-Hill Education 2002)
- The Art of Talking to Anyone: Essential People Skills for Success in Any Situation by Rosalie Maggio (McGraw Hill Higher Education 2005)
- How to Talk to Anyone: 92 Little Communication Tricks for Big Success in Relationships by Leil Lowndes (McGraw-Hill Contemporary 2003)
- Fierce Conversations: Achieving Success in Work and in Life, One Conversation at a Time by Susan Scott (Piatkus Books 2003)

Business Etiquette

On etiquette in general and business etiquette:
- Etiquette in Society, in Business, in Politics, and at Home by Emily Post (1922)
- Manners by Kate Spade (Simon & Schuster 2004)
- Power Etiquette: What You Don't Know Can Kill Your Career by Dana May Casperson (Amacom 1999)
- Talk to the Hand: The Utter Bloody Rudeness of Everyday Life (or Six Good Reasons to Stay Home and Bolt the Door) by Lynne Truss (Profile Books Ltd 2005)

- A Pinch of Posh: A Beginner's Guide to Being Civilised by Laurence Llewelyn-Bowen and Jacqueline Llewelyn-Bowen (Collins 2006)
- Jane Austen's Guide to Good Manners: Compliments, Charades and Horrible Blunders by Henrietta Webb and Josephine Ross (Bloomsbury Publishing 2006)
- A Modern Girl's Guide to Etiquette by Sarah Ivens (Piatkus Books 2003)
- Her Ladyship's Guide to Modern Manners by Lucy Gray and Robert Allen (National Trust Books 2006)
- Etiquette: Henry's Guide to Modern Manners by Henry Russell (Cassell Illustrated 2006)

Specifically on entertainment and social event (including dining etiquette)
- The Mere Mortal's Guide to Fine Dining: From Salad Forks to Sommeliers, How to Eat and Drink in Style Without Fear of Faux Pas by Colleen Rush (Broadway Books 2006)
- Emily Post's Favourite Party and Dining Tips: A Guide for Guests and Hosts by Peggy Post (HarperCollins 2005)
- Emily Post's Table Manners for Today: Advice for Every Dining Occasion by Elizabeth L. Post (HarperReference 1994)
- Miss Manners' Basic Training: Eating by Judith Martin (Crown Publications 1997)

How to become a partner

On career coaching for lawyers, see the articles and newsletters published by Ellen Ostrow Ph.D., who specialises in personal and career coaching for women lawyers (http://www.lawyerslifecoach.com)
On career coaching in general:
- The Coaching at Work Toolkit by Perry Zeus and Suzanne Skiffington (McGraw-Hill Publishing 2002)
- The Portable Mentor: Your Anytime, Anywhere Career Coach and Problem Solver by Cy Charney (Amacom 2003)
- Take Yourself to the Top: The Secrets of America's #1 Career Coach by Laura Berman-Fortgang (HarperCollins 1999)
- Your Coach (in a Book): the Ultimate Guide to Navigating the Trickiest Career, Leadership, and Business Challenges You Will Ever Face by Hargrove (Pfeiffer Wiley 2004)
- The Career Change Handbook: How to Find Out What You're Good at and What You Enjoy - Then Get Someone to Pay You for It by Graham Green (How To Books Ltd 2006)

- How to Get a Job You'll Love: A Practical Guide to Unlocking Your Talents and Finding Your Ideal Career by John Lees (McGraw-Hill Education 2004)
- Build Your Own Rainbow: Workbook for Career and Life Management by Barrie Hopson, Mike Scally, Hopson Barrie (Management Books 1999)
- From New Recruit to High Flyer: No-nonsense Advice on How to Fast Track Your Career by Hugh Karseras (Kogan Page Ltd 2006)
- Nice Girls Don't Get the Corner Office: 101 Unconscious Mistakes Women Make by Lois P. Frankel (Little, Brown & Company 2004)
- 50 Success Classics: Winning Wisdom For Work & Life From 50 Landmark Books by Tom Butler-Bowdon (Nicholas Brealey Publishing 2004)
- How to Become a CEO: The Rules for Rising to the Top of Any Organisation by Jeffrey J. Fox (Vermilion 2000)

On life coaching in general:
- Life Coaching for Dummies by Jeni Mumford (John Wiley and Sons Ltd 2006)
- The Worst-case Scenario Survival Handbook: Work (Worst-Case Scenario Survival Handbooks) by Joshua Piven and David Borgenicht (Chronicle Books 2003)
- 50 Self-help Classics: 50 Inspirational Books to Transform Your Life from Timeless Sages to Contemporary Gurus by Tom Butler-Bowdon (Nicholas Brealey Publishing Ltd 2003)

Specifically on office politics:
- The Way of the Rat: A survival guide to office politics by Joep P.M. Schrijvers (Cyan Books 2004)
- Office Politics: How Work Really Works by Guy Browning (Ebury Press 2006)
- 21 Dirty Tricks at Work: How to Win at Office Politics by Mike Phipps and Colin Gautrey (Capstone Publishing 2005)
- The Rules of Office Politics by Rob Yeung (Cyan Books 2006)
- Winning Office Politics: Dubrin's Guide for the 90's by Andrew J. DuBrin (Prentice Hall 1990)

Business Development

On business development, marketing and sales:
- Get Clients Now! 28-day Marketing Program for Professionals and Consultants by C.J. Hayden (Amacom 1999)

- Creating Rainmakers: The Manager's Guide to Training Professionals to Attract New Clients by F. Harding (John Wiley & Sons Inc 2006)
- The Sales Mentor: Professional Sales 101 & 102 for the Development Years by Bobby L. Butler (Trafford Publishing 2006)
- Selling Skills for Professionals by Kim Tasso (Thorogood 2000)
- Marketing Your Services: A Step-by-step Guide for Small Businesses and Professionals by Anthony O. Putman (John Wiley & Sons Inc 1990)
- How to Become a Rainmaker: The Rules for Getting and Keeping Customers and Clients by Jeffrey J. Fox (Vermilion 2001)
- How to Close Every Sale by Girard (Warner Books 1998)
- How to Get Clients by Jeff Slutsky and Marc Slutsky (Warner Books 1992)
- Perfect Pitch: The Art of Selling Ideas and Winning New Business by Jon Steel (John Wiley & Sons 2006)

Delegation

On delegation and project management:
- The Definitive Guide to Project Management: The Fast Track to Getting the Job Done on Time and on Budget by Sebastian Nokes, Ian Major, Alan Greenwood and Mark Goodman (Financial Times Prentice Hall 2003)
- Project Management for Dummies by Stanley Portney (Hungry Minds Inc. 2001)
- Real Delegation: How to Get People to Do Things for You - and Do Them Well by J.K. Smart (Prentice Hall 2002)
- Essential Delegation Skills by Carla L. Brown (Gower Publishing Limited 1997)
- If You Want It Done Right, You Don't Have to Do It Yourself: The Art of Effective Delegation by Donna M. Genett (Quill Driver Books 2003)
- 50 Minute: Delegation Skills for Leaders by R Finch (Course Technology 2005)

Public Speaking

On public speaking:
- Presenting to Win: The Art of Telling Your Story by Jerry Weissman (Prentice Hall 2006)
- Beyond Bullet Points: Using Microsoft Powerpoint to Create Presentations That Inform, Motivate and Inspire by C. Atkinson (Microsoft Press,U.S. 2005)

- Lend Me Your Ears: All You Need to Know About Making Speeches and Presentations by Max Atkinson (Vermilion 2004)
- Public Speaking and Presentations for Dummies (For Dummies) by Malcolm Kushner and Rob Yeung (John Wiley and Sons Ltd 2006)
- High Impact Speeches: How to Write and Deliver Words That Move Minds by Richard Heller (Prentice Hall 2002)
- 10 Days to More Confident Public Speaking by Princeton Language Institute and Lenny Laskowski (Warner Books 2001)

Time and Stress Management

On time management:
- Getting Things Done: The Art of Stress-free Productivity by David Allen (Piatkus Books 2002)
- Do It Tomorrow and Other Secrets of Time Management by Mark Forster (Hodder & Stoughton Religious 2006)
- Eat That Frog! 21 Great Ways to Stop Procrastinating and Get More Done in Less Time by Brian Tracy (Hodder & Stoughton 2004)
- Get Everything Done and Still Have Time to Play by Mark Forster (Help Yourself 2000)

On stress management:
- The Great Office Detox: Minimize Stress and Maximize Job Satisfaction by Dawna Walter (Michael Joseph Ltd 2007)
- The Inner Game of Work: Overcoming Mental Obstacles for Maximum Performance by W.Timothy Gallwey (Texere Publishing, US 2002)
- The Relaxation and Stress Reduction Workbook by Martha Davis, Elizabeth Robbins Eshelman and Matthew McKay (New Harbinger Publications 2000)
- Stress Management for Dummies by Allen Elkin (Hungry Minds Inc 1999